JOHN DEERE
Two-Cylinder Collectibles

Greg Stephen

MBI Publishing Company

First published in 2000 by MBI Publishing Company, 729 Prospect Avenue, PO Box 1, Osceola, WI 54020-0001 USA

© Greg Stephen, 2000

MBI Publishing Company books are also available at discounts in bulk quantity for industrial or sales-promotional use. For details write to Special Sales Manager at Motorbooks International Wholesalers & Distributors, 729 Prospect Avenue, PO Box 1, Osceola, WI 54020-0001 USA.

Library of Congress Cataloging-in-Publication Data
Stephen, Greg.
    John Deere two-cylinder collectibles / Greg Stephen.
        p. cm.—(Collectors' reference guide)
    Includes index.
    ISBN 0-7603-0750-4 (pb : alk. paper)
        1. John Deere tractors—Collectibles—Catalogs. I. Title.
        II. Series.
TL233.6.J64 S74   2000
631.3'72'075—dc21   00-030488

On the front cover: For more than 160 years, "John Deere" has symbolized the best in agricultural machinery. Today, collectors clamor to find artifacts, memorabilia, and collectibles associated with the company's products and history. Items in this collage are typical of the materials that draw enthusiasts to flea markets, swap meets, and deep into the barn in the hopes of uncovering a savory green and yellow relic. Items pictured include a 1938 sales catalog, several belt buckles, a Farmer's Notebook, a copy of Thresher, John Deere pencils, leaping deer lapel pin, wrench, factory badge, medallions, and the quintessential mark of one who "bleeds green," the John Deere cap. *Nick Cedar*
On the back cover: After you learn to recognize it, you will find that there is an unlimited amount of memorabilia associated with John Deere. Over the years, Deere & Company issued or approved a wide array of items ranging from drinking glasses and tools to volumes of printed literature, watch fobs, and home decorations. The key to forming a good collection is recognizing the vintage of the item and its relative scarcity.

All items pictured in *John Deere Two-Cylinder Collectibles* are from the author's collection unless otherwise indicated.

All photos by Cindy Stephen, unless otherwise noted.

Edited by John Adams-Graf
Designed by Tom Heffron

Printed in the United States of America

Contents

DEDICATION

The author wishes to dedicate this book to his family,
which bore up well while this project was being completed.
Thank you to my wife, Cindy,
and my two children still at home, Sean and Danny.

ACKNOWLEDGMENTS

T he author would like to sincerely thank the following people for their time and expertise in helping to make this book a reality: Robert Duffel, Iowa; Melvin and Annette Warren, Iowa; Dale Johnson, Minnesota; Kurt Aumann, Illinois; Bob Key, Colorado; and Dave Morrison, Colorado. Some suggested helpful changes, others verified information, and others simply listened. Several made their collections available for viewing and/or photographing. And to all the others not listed, a sincere thank-you,

—*Greg Stephen*

INTRODUCTION

John Deere—two simple words that elicit a veritable flood of imagery and emotion from generations of people the world over. For more than 160 years, John Deere has meant the absolute best in farm equipment to those who depend on it for their livelihood. More recently, John Deere–associated collectibles have created a new legion of enthusiasts. Why this fascination with a tractor and the name John Deere? One hundred sixty years after its founding, the John Deere Company remains independent and a world leader in producing agricultural equipment. Deere's consistent policy of producing reliable, quality equipment with the features desired by its customers soon led it to the top of the tractor industry. This was in no small part due to the famous John Deere Two-Cylinder tractors that were produced from 1923 until 1960. These tractors, even today, bear the enviable reputation of remarkable longevity and durability. Indeed, many are still on the job today earning their keep. Over the years, even while they were still being produced, admiration for their qualities led to people beginning to gather up one or two as a testament of their loyalty to the tractors that had served them so well. Steam engine and threshing shows began to appear, and some of these older John Deeres were tuned up and taken to a show. As with many things that are collected, one leads to another and soon older John Deeres were avidly sought out and taken home to swell burgeoning collections.

Indeed, a new sense of urgency had been imparted, as now there was a definite beginning and end to available John Deere two-cylinder tractors. The "nostalgia factor" must also be considered. An antique tractor brings with it thoughts and memories of a less complicated, less hurried era. Over time, the less common models of John Deeres began to rise in value. As values of rare variations of the tractors continued their explosive rise, an interesting facet of the hobby began to develop. Collectors began to seek out various original accessories, parts, and associated items that dealt with the tractors. Advertising pieces for their favorite tractors were a prime find. Parts and service manuals were a useful item to add to one's antique library. Uncommon options for a tractor were also chased after. Equipment that had been available when a tractor was manufactured was added to growing accumulations of vintage tractors. Eventually, literally everything that dealt with the John Deere two-cylinder tractors was, and still is, frantically hunted and collected. Although the collecting craze currently encompasses John Deere tractors built after 1960—even John Deere's line of Lawn & Garden equipment—the scope of this book confines itself only to those items produced during the years the two-cylinder tractor and the Waterloo Boy were manufactured.

The tractors themselves are not covered in this book—just the items deemed collectible to today's hobbyists. Furthermore, only items considered genuine John Deere are covered. Although countless unofficial items have been linked with the two-cylinder tractor, this book will cover only official John Deere–approved items. It can be difficult today to ascertain what was Deere "approved" and what was not, since Deere many times gave tacit approval to items. In many locations, there was not a major national sales company that could provide the "official" item to every dealer. Although Deere itself offered many of the items directly to dealers, some found it best to deal with a local specialty company, and many times Deere found that acceptable.

During the two-cylinder tractor time period with which this book deals, many of the different John Deere branches or houses acted almost autonomously, often developing advertising items unique to their trade area. This can be true even today. Internal Deere company promotions, an executive's pet project, or even items applicable only to a certain area of the nation can result in collectible items that might seldom be seen in most areas of the country.

Collecting can be described as gathering, amassing, accumulating, or concentrating. This would be a fair definition of the pursuits of today's collector of Deere memorabilia. The profile of today's hobbyist is quite varied, ranging from the long-time farmers who have used Deere's products and appreciate the company's legacy, corporate executives who grew up on a farm driving a John Deere tractor, Deere employees who have seen firsthand the effects Deere has had on the world, small business owners who make their living from supplying the needs of the Deere hobby, to speculators who gamble on the rise and fall of various Deere products and dream of that one "killer" find. All these people and many others can be found actively collecting John Deere today. The last ten years have seen an explosive surge in John Deere collecting and in the antique tractor hobby in general. No one could have predicted the new levels that collecting has attained. An entire vocabulary has even evolved to deal with descriptions of various items one might run across in this hobby. A useful glossary for collectors of all skill levels is included in this book.

The best advice for beginning collectors is to collect what they like. Many will settle in on one area of collecting and concentrate on it alone. Examples of this are toys (sometimes even down to collecting strictly one type, such as the Ertl Precision Series), parts catalogs, items pertaining to a John Deere tractor they own, items that used to be on the family farm or that their dad had, sales pamphlets, and many others. As a beginning collector gathers and learns more, he becomes an advanced collector. Advanced collectors usually have an extensive collection and have gathered up most readily available items. They are more willing to pay more for an item than a beginning collector would be. These expensive items are usually quite a bit harder to locate or were made in far fewer numbers. Advanced collectors are aware of this and have also risen to the level where they "need" these items for their collection to improve.

There is another category of collector who, some may say, is "over the edge" when it comes to collecting John Deere. These are the ones who collect every single thing that Deere has made: green, yellow, rusty, shiny, new, old, metal, paper, rare, or common—it does not matter to these collectors! These are the "extreme" collectors.

A collector who has the largest gathering of items assembled in the hobby and adds missing items as he runs across them is not an extreme collector, though he is perhaps an advanced collector. Extreme collectors have a "shotgun" approach to this hobby and gather anything and everything, usually with no direction or purpose behind their acquisitions. These are the most dangerous types to come up against in an auction, as their thirst for acquiring knows no bounds, and they are likely to drive an item's price far above what it would normally fetch. They can also be one of the most fun to watch as they happily bid their way to ownership of a new item. Extreme collecting is reckless and can be dangerous to the bank account as well.

Readers of this book are most likely already collectors themselves, or latent collectors about to blossom forth into full-fledged participation in this hobby. Many of you who are already collectors may find that you are far deeper into this hobby than you had thought. The almost endless variety of John Deere collectibles and memorabilia is what makes this hobby so very interesting and enjoyable.

A few final thoughts to the new collectors. An easy way to quickly determine if an item falls into the two-cylinder time frame is the John Deere logo itself. The glossary at the back covers this, but is worthwhile to mention here. If the item, be it a screwdriver or a piece of paper, has the four-legged deer logo, it is most likely from the two-cylinder tractor era. Also, be aware that even in this hobby unscrupulous people are out there who are just waiting to separate you from your money. There are growing numbers of reproduction items that, although nice, are not original and as such have no value as collectibles. Also, a few items may have been doctored or forged, which can be difficult to identify. A good rule of thumb is, if a supposedly rare item is available repeatedly or is offered at a "too good to be true" price, then there may be more to it than meets the eye.

All this being said, the John Deere collecting hobby is certainly one of the most enjoyable, fulfilling, and thrilling hobbies there is. This book was written to facilitate an understanding of what the hobby is and to raise the level of knowledge of what is available. Of course, not every item can be listed, and the pricing guide is just that, a general guide. There will be variations up and down on these and other items. New items continue to surface every week. Use what is presented in this book as you see fit and enjoy!

PRICING GUIDE

The following pages present a wide variety of John Deere collectibles from all areas of collecting organized into categories to facilitate comparisons and reference. Several areas need to be addressed concerning the pricing guide. No attempt has been made to cover every collectible made by Deere during the two-cylinder era. There are just too many objects to list. Some of these items are also extremely difficult to locate today or are in advanced collections and unavailable to most collectors. Additionally, many items are not known about; even today, new ones continue to be uncovered all the time. Efforts to cover all of the two-cylinder era collectibles will continue to be an ongoing process. This, of course, is part of the appeal to the hobbyist.

No single collector can ever say that he has every two-cylinder era collectible ever produced, as they have not all been discovered. As the hobby has grown and new people have entered into collecting, the idea of what is collectible has also changed. Traditionally, items that were collected have been parts catalogs, sales literature, dealer's sales catalogs, toys, promotional and advertising items, and the tractors themselves. Today, all these items are collected as well as new and nontraditional collectibles such as carburetors, steel wheels, original packaging for parts, Deere corporate items, letters and correspondence, service bulletins, boxes that toys came in, print advertisements or signage for the toys, displays for vintage parts and tractors, dealership shelving and displays, tractor special tools, magnetos, Deere factory employee items, press kits, and more and more all the time. Today it can truly be said that if Deere made it, endorsed it, had one of its products or its name featured on it, was affiliated with it, or in any manner was connected with it, or if the item had any green on it, then it is collected by someone somewhere.

The values that are listed herein are also intended only as a guideline. They have been culled from auctions, private sales, information provided by collectors, and historical values. Recently, many items have sold for far more than what was believed to be their value, some items bringing almost unbelievable prices. A collector needs to be aware of the underlying forces and developing trends that are driving this upward spiral in pricing. Primarily, the John Deere collectibles hobby is maturing. After the hobby's growing at a phenomenal rate, many collectors have been in it long enough that they have filled out their collections and are now concentrating on more elusive items for them. These same collectors have availed themselves of any information that they have had access to, thereby increasing their knowledge of the rarity of certain collectibles.

Hobby magazines such as *Green Magazine*, *Two Cylinder*, *Belt Pulley*, *Antique Power*, and brand-specific magazines have gone a long way toward distributing general collectible awareness. Increasing numbers of collectors desirous of owning items that are in finite supply result in higher prices. Over and above these factors the economy has been abnormally strong in recent years, giving hobbyists more disposable income.

Rising values make it difficult to pin down what an item is worth, especially since no one knows where the price spiral will end. A new and seldom considered development promises, I think, to change the face of collecting forever. Everyone today is familiar with the Internet, and it has rapidly become the driving force for our future. We all face Internet-entwined advertising every day, and it seems as if the Internet affects every area of our existence. John Deere collectors are also confronted with the convergence of vintage items colliding with the cyber culture of today's daily life. At first glance, it would not appear that computers have any impact on items produced decades before it came into existence, but don't forget the awesome effects online auctions such as those on eBay, Yahoo, Amazon, and other sites have had on collectibles in general. Traditional auction fare such as glassware, dolls, guns, and the like have all found an enthusiastic reception in the new venue of online auctions. John Deere and other farm-related items are no exception. Where once a collector had to contend with a crowd of several hundred potential competitors when attempting to purchase an article at an auction, today he must literally vie with everyone in the world when a desired piece is offered up online.

What does all this mean to the collector? Well, the seller will certainly benefit as selling prices are maximized from the surge of qualified and interested bidders that will be participating in these auctions via simulcast and online bidding. So on that far date in the future when a collection is dispersed, for whatever reason, it will realize realistic proceeds. Granted, most truly valuable items will bring far more post-Internet than they might have pre-Internet. This is not entirely a bad thing for a collector, as true values will become established for genuine rare pieces. Most likely, pricing and availability trends will be charted, thereby allowing more pricing information to be offered to both buyers and sellers alike. This will enable a collector to make an intelligent purchasing decision. This information is offered up to today's collector in the hope that all of these factors will be thought of when building a collection. Keep this in mind when studying the value guides that follow and remember, an informed collector is a successful collector.

CHAPTER 1

OPERATORS' MANUALS

John Deere wanted to make sure that each owner of a piece of John Deere equipment knew that only genuine parts fit and functioned like the originals. As can be imagined, even more than repair parts catalogs, operator's manuals were used to convey this message and used often. It was not uncommon for the manual to make the rounds of a field while residing in the tractor's toolbox. Of course, the toolbox was also usually home to oil cans, pliers, miscellaneous broken parts, and lots and lots of wire. Add in the odd nail, interesting rock, and greasy farmer's fingers and it is easy to see that the operator's

This model 40 tractor operator's manual is not only still in its original dark water-resistant envelope, it has never been opened! A great find!

manual was usually the worse for wear after a few summers. More than a few decades of age also contributed to the disintegration of the paper itself and today some manuals are all but impossible to decipher.

Luckily, Deere still reprints most operator's manuals but, of course, these do not suit the purpose of the collector. While a reprint is usually sufficient for a restorer's needs, a collector is interested only in obtaining original operator's manuals that were printed at or near the time of the tractor's production. Early operator's manuals were little more than lightweight paper booklets, as the early machines were not as complicated as later ones would be.

As equipment increased in sophistication and complexity, the operator's manual was also revised to reflect the new features that were being added. Advances in engineering and farming practices also engendered changes in farm equipment. More-durable covers were added to operator's manuals to aid in their survival in customers' hands. Early manuals bore black-and-white prints of machines, while later manuals sported color covers and photographs of the equipment.

A final area of interest to collectors that was not foreseen by Deere are the quick scribblings often entered into the manual. If one is lucky enough to purchase a piece of equipment from the original owner and obtain the original manual, quite often the farmer will have entered the unit's serial number, date of purchase, and other interesting facts that help fill out the history of a machine.

Later operator's manuals even began to be shipped in watertight dark brown envelopes. These are highly prized if still intact, as the operator's manual will have been protected more than is usual, and most envelopes were discarded soon after a machine was delivered. There has been a definite increase in the last several years in the prices paid for original operator's manuals. If collectors were simply after the information contained within, then current reprints would sell for as much as originals. This is not the case, so one is left to draw the conclusion that collectors are expanding their efforts in preserving the past—even into the area of original operator's manuals.

Prices (note: all manuals are originals, not reprints)

Item	Price
Manual, operator's, Model #5 mower, OMH10156, #6	$10.00
Manual, operator's, Model 116W baler, OME1255, #5	8.00
Manual, operator's, Model 15 subsoiler, OMW18954, #6	10.00
Manual, operator's, Model 320 tractor, OMT43757, 76 pp, #6	31.00
Manual, operator's, Model 330 tractor, OMT59558, #8	76.00
Manual, operator's, Model 40 tractor, OMT6423, 100 pp, #5	41.00
Manual, operator's, Model 420 tractor, OMT4737, 80 pp, #5	25.00
Manual, operator's, Model 44 plow, OMA1352, #6	10.00
Manual, operator's, Model 520 tractor, OMR2074, 108 pp, #6	24.00
Manual, operator's, Model 55/95/105 combines, OMH66416, #3	5.00
Manual, operator's, Model 620 tractor, OMR2078, 108 pp, #6	29.00

Another great manual, this Waterloo Boy tractor operator's manual is dated March 1, 1918, and has seen little use. Words to the wise were printed at the bottom "STUDY THIS BOOK IT WILL SAVE YOU TIME AND TROUBLE." Helpful advice if it were taken.

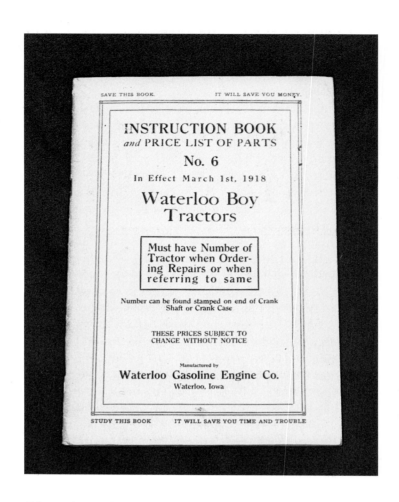

Prices *(note: all manuals are originals, not reprints)*

Item	Price
Manual, operator's, Model 7 Sheller, OMC10651, #8	$10.00
Manual, operator's, Model 720 tractor, OMR2086, 108 pp, #7	25.00
Manual, operator's, Model 77 Duster, OMD11148, #8	10.00
Manual, operator's, Model 810 plow, OMA71157, 24 pp, #5	21.00
Manual, operator's, Model B drill, OMM1947, 30 pp, #6	7.00
Manual, operator's, Model BR/BO tractor, OMRBR1, #6	35.00
Manual, operator's, Model D tractor, DIR225, #9	65.00
Manual, operator's, Model GP tractor, DIR104, #4	50.00
Manual, operator's, Model GP tractor, DIR104, #8	85.00
Manual, operator's, Model H spreader, OMC11247, 51 pp, #7	10.00
Manual, operator's, Model H spreader, OMC1651, #5	5.00
Manual, operator's, Model H tractor, OMR3011R, 68 pp, #6	32.00
Manual, operator's, Model LA tractor, DIR207, #8	55.00
Manual, operator's, Model M1/M2 plow, OMA111151, #8	20.00
Manual, operator's, Waterloo Boy tractor, manual #7, 58 pages, #7	100.00
Manual, operator's, Model L tractor, DIR206, #7	45.00

CHAPTER 2

SERVICE MANUALS

Vintage service manuals, or technical manuals, as they are also known, can quite often be the saving factor in a restoration of an antique piece of equipment. The people who originally dealt with the antique machinery are becoming quite scarce, so it is up to the individual collector to answer his own questions. Service manuals are a great source of information on maintaining the older equipment. Paper collectors also collect them due to their age and scarcity. Most period manuals were used and handled frequently; therefore, many bear at least a few greasy fingerprints or notes written in the margins. While this does add a certain charm to the piece, it also ensures that service manuals in excellent condition will bring higher prices. John Deere currently reprints many of these service

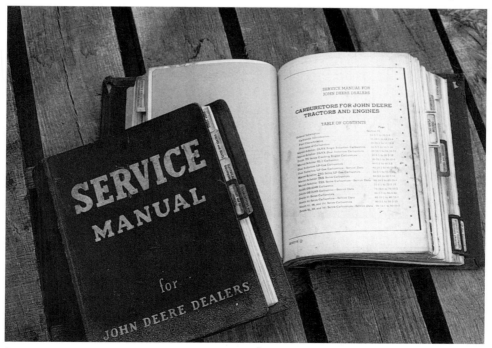

Service manuals nearly always suffered the results of being utilized in a repair shop where conditions were not necessarily the most sanitary. Most original service manuals today bear grease, paint, and pencil marks. Shown is the Carburetor Service Manual for Tractors and Engines. The pictured service manuals are still in the binder that they came in, complete with dividing tabs. A very hard-to-find item today.

The "Tractors and Engines-General" service manual was usually the first one in the service manual binder. It covered basic information about tractors and their construction.

texts, so the collector must educate himself to ensure that he is buying a true vintage manual and not a reprint.

Collectors interested in the information in a service manual can often make do with a reprint but most prefer to have the original. Of course, most tractors were covered in detail in service manuals, but there were exceptions. Despite rumors to the contrary, positive proof of a John Deere service manual for the following tractors has not been located: Model A, unstyled Model B, Model C, Model D (with the exception noted below), Model G, Model GP (with the exception noted below), Model H, Model L, and Model LA. Exceptions to the above are as follows: "Tractors & Engines Service Manual," published in 1929, covers the basics of the very early unstyled Model D, Model GP, and Type E engines.

Deere also produced service manuals on separate systems of tractors and machines such as Carburetion, Electrical Systems, LP Fuel Systems, PowrTrol, Hydraulics, and Power Steering. These systems were all judged important enough to warrant the production of a manual specific to each. These technical manuals contained detailed in-depth information on servicing each type of system. Troubleshooting information was also available and more than once saved the day for the technician. Also, since tractor-related items are valued more highly in general, collectors should keep their eyes open when searching for a new acquisition. Tractor service manuals and, to a lesser degree, implement service manuals are well worth collecting.

Prices *(note: all manuals are originals, not reprints)*

Item	Price
Manual, service, "John Deere Tractors & Engines," dated 1928, #8	$85.00
Manual, service, Carburetors, SM2024, #9	75.00
Manual, service, Fuel Injection Pumps, SM2045, #8	75.00
Manual, service, GM-253 engine (435 tractor), SM2028, #6	45.00
Manual, service, Hydraulic equipment, SM2011, #7	40.00
Manual, service, LP gas equipment, SM2015, #9	40.00
Manual, service, Model 40 tractor, SM2013, #7	65.00
Manual, service, Model 50 tractor, SM2006, #9	50.00
Manual, service, Model 60 tractor, SM2008, #8	55.00
Manual, service, Model 70 diesel tractor, SM2017, #6	55.00
Manual, service, Model 720 diesel tractor, SM2020, #7	65.00
Manual, service, Model 720 gas tractor, SM2025, #6	35.00
Manual, service, Model 820 diesel tractor, SM2021, #8	65.00
Manual, service, Model M tractor, SM2001, #8	65.00
Manual, service, Model R tractor, SM2005, #7	75.00
Manual, service, Power Lifts, old, #8	35.00
Manual, service, Power Steering, SM2050, #8	50.00
Manual, service, PowrTrol, SM2022, #8	35.00

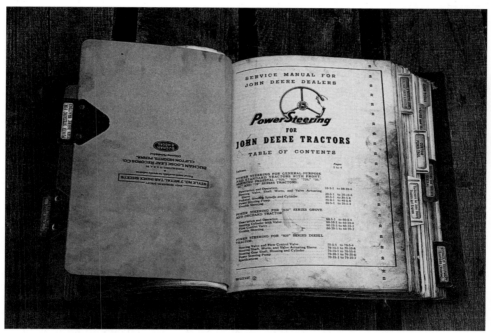

"Power Steering for John Deere Tractors" was a popular manual in every shop. This popularity was due to the difficulty in servicing the power steering systems on two-cylinder tractors. Just how popular this manual was is evident by the heavy soiling on its edge. The troubleshooting charts inside facilitated countless repairs.

Chapter 3

Parts Catalogs

O ne of the more useful and impressive items to collectors are Deere's repair parts catalogs. As long as there has been a John Deere company, there has been a need for parts to repair its machines. Parts catalogs for implements originated long ago, and the catalogs for the tractors made their debut with the arrival of Deere's own tractor line in 1923. Early catalogs were, and still are, quite remarkable due to their style of construction. They were usually bound in groups of related machines and had thick paper covers and cloth-covered spines. Factor in the liberal amount of printing on the covers and the spine and a collection of vintage parts catalogs can look very imposing on a bookshelf. But the real value of a collection of parts catalogs is in the information they contain. This information can sometimes be found nowhere else and is of inestimable value to a person performing a restoration of a vintage piece of equipment.

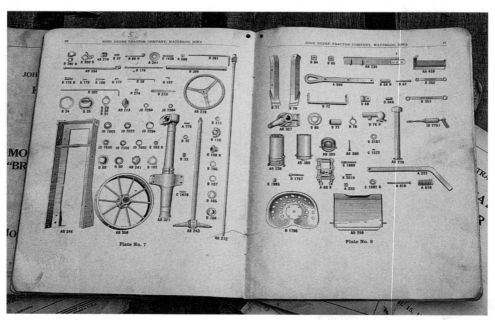

The exploded parts views of the model B tractor are beautifully rendered. Every part is illustrated clearly, a great help in restoration. Astute collectors will notice that the four-bolt pedestal is shown; after it was updated to an eight-bolt pedestal, later catalogs no longer listed the earlier four-bolt version.

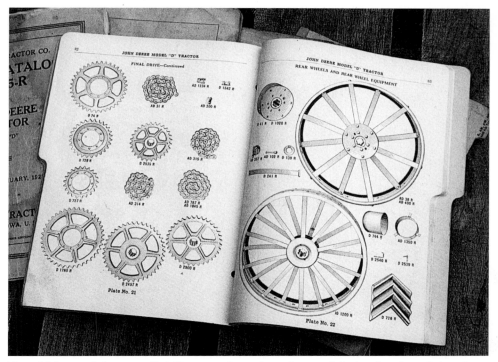

The model D tractor had numerous final drive gear options and several rear steel-wheel configurations, all shown here.

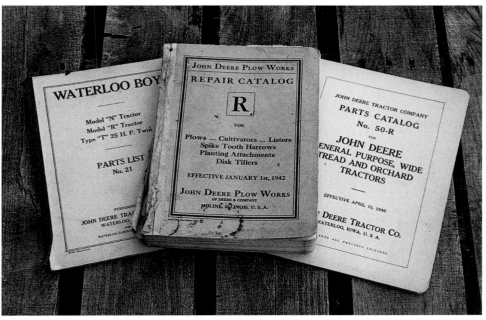

Three more uncommon parts catalogs. The middle one, the "R" plow works repair catalog, is more than 1,000 pages and covers nearly all early plows made by Deere. Priceless information. The catalog on the left is a Waterloo Boy catalog, while the one on the right covers the model GP tractor and is dated 1940.

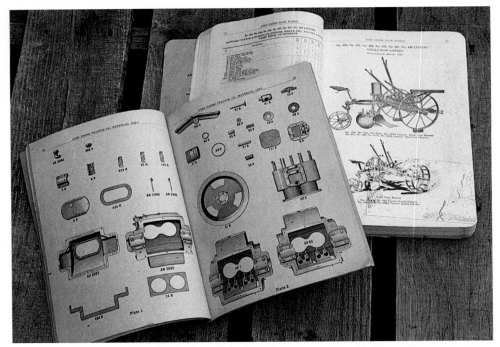

The great illustrations are again shown, this time of the Waterloo Boy tractor and one from the "R" Plow Works catalog.

A glance inside a parts catalog is like a walk back in time, to when the equipment was new. To a collector, a parts catalog that was published at the same time as his machine is the only vehicle for determining exactly what parts are correct for it. The illustrations in the catalog may be the only clue to locating or reproducing a missing part. There may also not be any other reference to a part on a vintage tractor except its listing in the "period" catalog. Later parts catalogs usually contain numerous revisions and updates. As updated catalogs were issued, the normal course of action was to update the parts library, and older versions of catalogs were usually thrown away. This means that it can be quite a hunt to locate a correct "period" catalog for, say, a 1925 John Deere Model D tractor.

The best advice one can offer a collector or restorer is, if you are looking for a particular catalog and one becomes available, just buy it. It is far better to have the information contained inside it than to sit wishing you had it for months to come. Advanced collectors attempt to collect all versions of a parts catalog. Luckily, the catalogs are rarely updated once the machine they refer to passes out of production. There is usually one final revision and that version serves as the final parts catalog for that machine. The less frequently a catalog is updated, the fewer versions there are to hunt out.

Parts catalogs, especially for tractors, endured some of the roughest treatment there was to be had. It also seems that the very paper they were printed on is somewhat less stable than other publications. As such, the vintage parts catalog is usually in poor condition. That is why a seldom-used original catalog will command a premium price.

Prices *(note: all catalogs are original, not reprints)*

Item	Price
Catalog, parts, JD Model 55 combine, combo parts/instruction manual, #PLH13551, #6	$9.00
Catalog, parts, 1926–1929 cornpickers, PCN9, #8	10.00
Catalog, parts, Dain Hay Machinery, #103-E, 564 pp, 1941, #8	35.00
Catalog, parts, Deere & Mansur Works, #21B, 731 pp, 1939, #7	25.00
Catalog, parts, Deere & Mansur Works, #22B, 509 pp, 1942, #6	20.00
Catalog, parts, JD Wagon Works, Rotary Hoes/Rod Weeders, #11D, 28 pp, 1930, #7	15.00
Catalog, parts, Model 1/1A corn sheller, PC155, #9	15.00
Catalog, parts, Model 1/A1/B1 plow, PC195, #8	20.00
Catalog, parts, Model 25 loader, PC254, #7	8.00
Catalog, parts, Model 4 mower, PCH69, #7	10.00
Catalog, parts, Model 87 sweep rake, PC154, #7	8.00
Catalog, parts, Model GP tractor, #50R, #9	75.00
Catalog, parts, Model L tractor, PC150, #9	65.00
Catalog, parts, Model LA tractor, PC151, #9	65.00
Catalog, parts, Plow Works, Plows/Cultivators/Planting, #Q, 1,311 pp, #8	185.00
Catalog, parts, Plow Works, Plows/Cultivators/Planting, #R, 1,165 pp, 1942, #7	150.00
Catalog, parts, Tractors & Engines, #45R, 1936, 388 pp, #8	100.00
Catalog, parts, Tractors & Engines, #45R, 1936, 388 pp, #4	55.00
Catalog, parts, Waterloo Boy Tractor Model N, #F40, 80 pp, 1920, combo parts catalog and price list, #8	100.00
Catalog, parts, Waterloo Boy Tractor Model N, #F51, 58 pp, 1920, combo parts/instruction manual #7, #7	100.00
Catalog, parts, Waterloo Boy Tractor Model N/R, stationary engine type T, #F75, 90 pages, 1926, parts catalog #21, #8	100.00

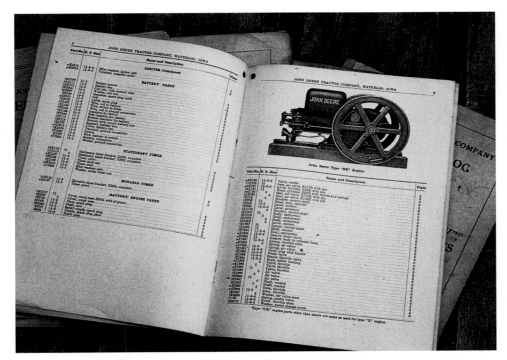

Even the diminutive-type "E" flywheel engine had its own catalog.

CHAPTER 4

SPECIAL PARTS CATALOGS AND ORDERS FOR REPAIRS

Anyone who has ever sold parts knows that there are always certain items that sell more frequently than others. These are known as fast-moving parts—usually maintenance items such as filters, grease, and oil or parts that wear out or break frequently, requiring constant replacement. Deere discovered long ago that it was much more efficient to group these parts into a handy quick reference booklet that would save the parts personnel valuable time. By assembling certain types of parts into a special book, Deere was able to provide these commonly needed parts to the customer faster and with a greater degree of accuracy. These included sweeps, hay cutting parts, chain and chain repair links, hardware and hardware items, plow shares, and more

Deere also found that increased sales resulted from including select parts that were commonly purchased on impulse. These were listed where a parts person who used the

These Special Parts Catalogs date from the 1930s and 1940s. The bright red covers have survived better on some than others. The Orders for Repairs feature a smaller format and various color covers. All catalogs pictured prominently display the "Roman" John Deere, complete with toga!

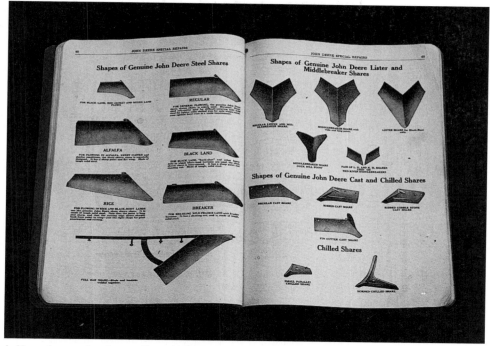

Inside, partsmen and customers alike could find commonly needed tillage parts.

book would not fail to notice them and might attempt to sell them to a customer. Umbrellas, umbrella brackets, sickle repair tools, hand tools, grease guns, and in later years, even toys, were all included in the quick reference guide. These books numbered, at least in the earlier versions, somewhere around 100 pages, and during the 1930s and 1940s they were softbound in a bright red color to enable them to be easily located.

These catalogs can also be an invaluable aid in identifying mislabeled parts. The changes a part went through as time passed is clearly documented in these interesting little books. Later editions grew in size and number of parts listed, and this only increases their desirability to today's collector.

Another neat little book was the "Order for Repairs & Extras" booklets that Deere published to allow dealers to place orders for commonly needed parts. These booklets are very similar to the Special Parts Catalogs in that there are some limited pictures and explanations of some parts. They differ in that they are not a reference catalog, but rather an order form that the dealer used to replenish his stock on a scheduled basis. The booklet was used also as a parts contract between the dealer and John Deere. The dealer retained a copy of the booklet for his records after he and Deere's agent signed it. It is interesting to note that there were really not that many parts that were deemed necessary at this point in time and the parts that were listed were listed by the machine they fit. A quick study of the machines listed gives today's enthusiast an overview of which ones were important to Deere, the dealer, and the farmer.

These 1935 and 1936 Orders for Repairs are in good shape for their age. Both have the word "copy" penciled in the upper corner, as these were no doubt the dealer's copy.

John Deere was dedicated to promoting the idea of customer confidence, as seen on the back of this later catalog. Two books to aid in the design and layout of the parts department were announced. That all-important word "Profit" was sure to get the dealer's attention!

Prices

Item	Price
Catalog, Special Parts/Price List, 1946, 129 pp, #7	$25.00
Catalog, Special Parts/Price List, 1947, 130 pp, #5	20.00
Catalog, Special Parts/Price List, 1949, 114 pp, #5	20.00
Catalog, Special Repairs/Price List, 1933, 133 pp, #7	30.00
Catalog, Special Repairs/Price List, 1934, 141 pp, #7	30.00
Catalog, Special Repairs/Price List, 1935, 138 pp, #8	25.00
Catalog, Special Repairs/Price List, 1940, 137 pp, #7	25.00
Catalog, Special Repairs/Price List, 1944, 137 pp, #7	25.00
Catalog, Special Repairs/Price List, 1945, 132 pp, #8	25.00
Order, Repairs & Extras, Omaha Branch, 1922, 16 pp, #8	25.00
Order, Repairs & Extras, Omaha Branch, 1935, 112 pp, #7	25.00
Order, Repairs & Extras, Omaha Branch, 1936, 116 pp, #7	25.00
Order, Repairs & Extras, Omaha Branch, 1940, 136 pp, #6	25.00

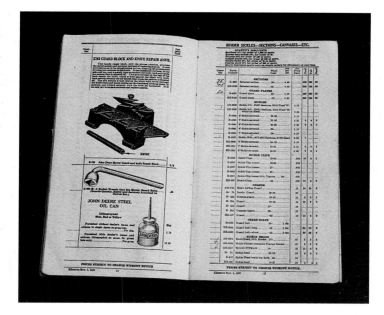

Handy tools like mower sickle repair blocks, wrenches, and even oil cans were all listed in Special Parts Catalogs, making them a great identification resource for todayís collectors.
Greg Stephen

John Deere did not waste the backs of the Special Repairs Catalogs. This one stressed the advantages of utilizing the pictured modern parts bins.

CHAPTER 5

SERVICE AND SALES BULLETINS

In the long ago days before the world was "wired," there was not a ready means to quickly address either service- or sales-related issues. The normal procedure during this time was to print up bulletins as necessary that would detail instructions on how to deal with these matters. Sales bulletins are interesting to a collector as they provide a window into the evolution of John Deere equipment. Sales bulletins announced everything from the introduction of a new implement to a new cigar lighter for a tractor. As such, they are invaluable when collectors attempt to pinpoint exact dates that certain options first became available or even when they were discontinued. The bulletins also announced changes in equipment pricing, personnel, parts, and company information. Service bulletins currently occupy the major portion of a collector's interest as they deal hands on, so to speak, with the actual machinery. Engine modifications, durability issues, proper operation procedures, constant stressing of safety and operator education, product improvements to correct a deficiency, general shop education, even holiday greetings are all to be found in these captivating documents. And every so often, Deere printed a "Red Face Department" notice in a bulletin when information that was printed in an earlier bulletin was found to be wrong!

The service bulletins also covered such topics as warranty coverage, new machinery specifications, service item suggestions such as lubricants and chemicals, suggested service shop

An assortment of service bulletins from the 1950s.

promotions to bring in new business, service shop layout and design, and, of interest to today's Deere tool collectors, introduction of new service tools. Collectors of John Deere cans and boxes are not left out either, as the service bulletins have great pictures of the actual products themselves in their packaging, and this can serve to date when a particular can or package was first introduced.

Enthusiasts in all areas of John Deere collecting can appreciate the great pictures of the tractors and implements that can be found in nearly every service bulletin. These service bulletins were issued monthly with interim ones as necessary. Interestingly, there is not known to be a complete set of Deere service bulletins. Currently, the earliest known issues date to the early 1930s but their numbering confirms that earlier bulletins were printed. The problem with locating every service bulletin is that although every John Deere dealer received the service bulletins, and does to this day in some form, most were discarded long ago. It probably seemed pointless to most dealers to continue to shelve books full of old bulletins that had not been looked at in years when the very equipment covered by these bulletins had mostly been consigned to the fencerow.

The best source for service bulletins would be a dealership that has been in business basically unchanged for many years. Of course, of those few, most will not part with the bulletins anyway. The collector is left with online auctions and hobby publications to attempt to gather up both service and sales bulletins. The effort is worth it though, as these are perhaps the most interesting paper collectibles Deere ever made.

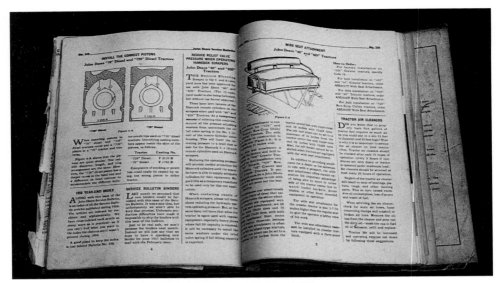

This bulletin dealt with a wide seat attachment for the model 40 and 420 tractors.

Prices

Item	Price
Bulletin, service #106-S, Feb. 1940, 4 pp, dealer success story, #6	$5.00
Bulletin, service #55-S, Nov. 1935, 4 pp, Tools/A,B,D tractor, #8	5.00
Bulletin, service #68-S, Dec. 1936, 4 pp, Xmas/Shop procedures, #8	8.00
Bulletin, service , #165-S, Nov. 1949, 4 pp, A tractor/Manifolds/Pistons, #7	8.00
Bulletin, service , #177-S, March 1951, 4 pp, R tractor info/Oil, #8	5.00
Bulletin, service, #111-S, July 1940, 4 pp, Tire/PTO specs, #8	5.00
Bulletin, service, #121-S, May 1941, 10 pp, Tractor Specs/Tire Specs, #6	10.00
Bulletin, service, #150-S, Jan. 1945, 4 pp, Tractor wiring schematics, #8	15.00
Bulletin, service, #159-S, Jan. 1948, 8 pp, Wico X Magneto service, #8	20.00
Bulletin, service, #183-S, Sept. 1951, 4 pp, Special tools/MC tractor, #8	12.00
Bulletin, service, #196, Oct. 1952, 8 pp, Track Pads/Balers/Decals, #6	6.00
Bulletin, service, #203, May 1953, 8 pp, 40 tractor specs/attachments, #7	8.00
Bulletin, service, #209, Nov. 1953, 6 pp, LP tractor/R flywheel/tools, #7	8.00
Bulletin, service, #285, Jan. 1960, 6 pp, 45 dealer/840 tractor/Generator, #7	8.00
Bulletin, service, #69-S, Jan. 1937, 4 pp, Magneto/Tools, #8	20.00
Bulletin, service, #85-S, May 1938, 4 pp, A,B,G tractor/Magneto/Tools, #7	15.00
Bulletin, service, #95-S, March 1939, 4 pp, A,B,D,G,GP,H specs, #8	10.00
Bulletin, service, #97-S, May 1939, 4 pp, H tractor info., #7	15.00
Bulletin, service, 1945, 2 pp, Allied valve lifter, picture B tractor, #9	8.00
Bulletin, service, 1945, 4 pp, Budget "A" frame, picture A tractor, #9	5.00
Bulletin, service, 1945, 4 pp, Curtis air compressors, picture A tractor, #9	8.00
Bulletin, service, 1946, 4 pp, Black & Decker tools, picture A tractor, #9	8.00
Bulletin, service, 1948, 8 pp, Cormann-Rupp tire-filling pumps, tractors, #9	8.00
Bulletin, service, 1949, 4 pp, Sioux Tools, picture R tractor, #9	8.00
Bulletin, service, 1951, 2 pp, Bear steering tools, picture AR tractor, #9	8.00
Bulletin, service, 1951, 4 pp, Lincoln welders, picture B/GP tractor, #9	8.00
Bulletin, service, 1951, 8 pp, OTC hydraulic pullers, #9	5.00

CHAPTER 6

SALES BROCHURES
AND
CATALOGS

N earli every industry engaged in marketing a product has
found it advantageous to provide to customer prospects
an information-packed leaflet of some kind that allows the
potential buyer to learn more about a particular product.
John Deere provided these from the earliest years at no cost

Four colorful sales brochures evoke vivid images of the machinery they advertised. The models A, B, G, and GP tractors and the W power unit are all shown. The condition of these brochures is very good.

Tractors were not the only equipment meriting their own brochures. Shown here are the 55 combine, No. 4 mower, hammer mill and hay rake, and the 14T baler.

to inquirers. Prominent ads in newspapers and trade publications entreated readers to send for more information on the product being advertised. Deere passed along to area dealers the names of those farmers who wrote soliciting a brochure. The dealer, in turn, would contact the farmer and arrange a visit, usually bringing along additional sales information. In this fashion, the farmer had available everything Deere could supply him to assist in making his decision, hopefully a "green" decision.

The most common brochures usually consisted of six pages in a fold-open design. Some were even printed with an area for the address. Many larger surviving brochures have

The model AR tractor had a small bifold brochure, while the Modern Farming catalogs listed nearly all the equipment Deere offered. These are a great resource for restorers. The catalog on the right is very unusual. It is a salesman's reference catalog for the W power unit.

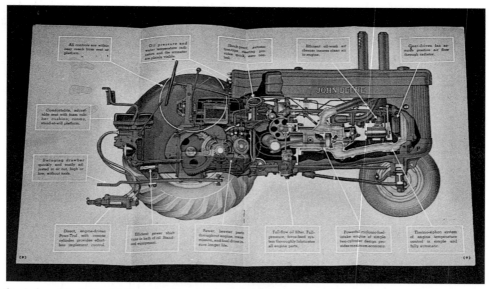

One look says it all. Great foldouts like this not only pointed out the features of the tractor in question but were likely responsible for the brochure escaping the garbage pail. Many times these colorful cutaway pictures were removed from the brochure they came in and were framed.

been folded in half, although that does not detract greatly from their value.

Other sales brochures were literally full-line catalogs and could number in the hundreds of pages. Smaller brochures were usually a one- or two-color effort. Color was used on the covers and in full-color gatefolds of featured items in the larger catalogs. These gatefolds, many, again, being large fold-open pictures, are quite stunning and add considerably to the value of a catalog. Although the artwork alone is striking, the collector can also find considerable value in studying these pictures when attempting a restoration of a similar machine. The catalogs provided complete specifications of the equipment and usually some pictures of the item in use. This answered the farmer's questions as to size, weight, capacity, and other essentials and also showed him what the machine could do if used in his field. Owner testimonials were sprinkled liberally throughout.

Another great attention-getter. The "Power" graphic above the model D tractor ensures that the brochure is read. Other great early advertising brochures include the early sales catalog on the left with the beautiful artwork of a little girl waving to her father in the field and what is surely one of the very first advertising brochures on the new "spoker" model D tractor on the right. All are exceedingly difficult to locate today.

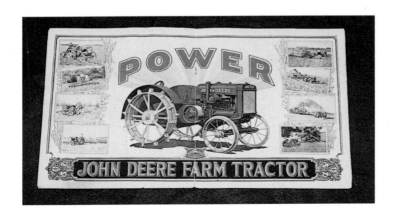

Another view of the "Power" model D tractor brochure.

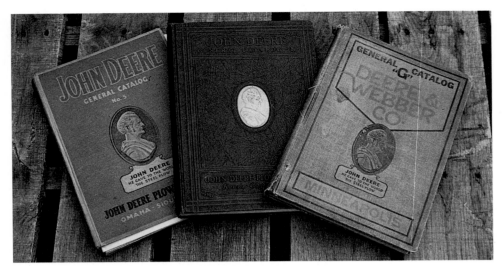

General Sales Catalogs look as impressive as the information they contain. The Omaha #5 catalog on the left retains more color than its Deere & Webber "G" catalog on the right. Cloth covered, these types of manuals were very susceptible to scuffing and wear. The "K" catalog in the center is one of the more highly sought-after general sales catalogs. Its embossed or tooled cover is as much the reason as the extensive information it contains.

Nearly all sales catalogs featured attractive designs. As they contained no pricing information, they were meant to be used for several years. The top catalog has a logo printed in gold of a deer leaping over a log. The bottom catalog is a Canadian version and is labeled Winnipeg Catalog "B" 1918.

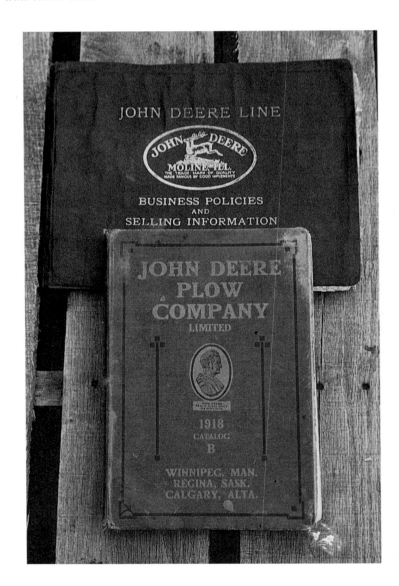

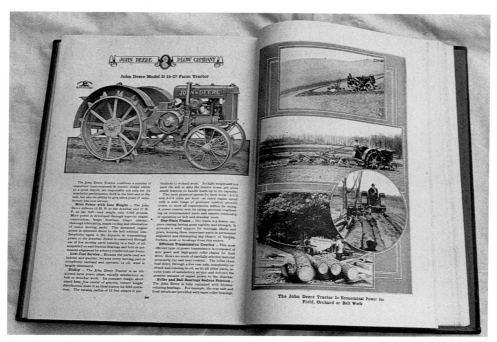

A sample page from a catalog lists all relevant information on the "spoker" model D tractor. What better guide for a restoration could there be?

Of particular interest to collectors today are the tractor-oriented pamphlets and catalogs, although this is changing slightly as interest increases in other equipment besides tractors. As there is generally less information available on equipment besides tractors, the sales pamphlets are becoming a worthy addition to a restorer's library. One of the most sought-after items in this category is anything related to a new model introduction. Introductory sales information, dealer introductory advertising kits, and farmer mailings are all highly collectible. Another valuable and rarely encountered item is the dealer's racks that held and displayed the sales pamphlets. There are various styles of these that changed through the years, and not many have survived to this day. Early racks were constructed

This is it. The most interesting catalog ever produced by Deere on the two-cylinder tractors. Inside, all conceivable information and specifications were listed. Indeed, the entire production of a two-cylinder tractor is covered from start to finish. Beautiful transparencies list each system of a two-cylinder tractor and lie over one another, making a tractor. A fantastic piece and nearly impossible to find today.

The A, G, BR, D, AOS tractors and others are all covered in the Two Cylinder Design catalog.

of wood while later ones were made of steel. Racks made even later routinely comprised plastic and steel components. Most of these racks are highly collectible themselves and make a great addition to display of a collection.

Prices

Item	Price
Cataglog, sales, "Two-Cylinder Design" presentation catalog, Models A/AR/AOS/B/BR/BO/D/G/H/L specific, numerous cutaway views, specifications, transparencies, and pictures. Very desirable two-cylinder tractor collectible, 110 pp, 1940s, #9	$850.00
Brochure, rack, metal green w/ 4-legged logo, full of sales brochures dating from 1915–1926, #8	2500.00
Brochure, rack, metal, black w/ 4-legged logo, #8	250.00
Brochure, rack, metal, double-sided free standing, green w/ 4-legged logo, #7	850.00
Brochure, rack, metal, green w/ 4-legged logo, #8	250.00
Brochure, rack, wooden w/ 4-legged logo, #6	100.00
Brochure, sales, "What the Haymakers Say," hay rake, 16 pp, 1930, #6	25.00
Brochure, sales, 30 series tractors, 15 pp, 1958, #8	85.00
Brochure, sales, Hammer Mills, 16 pp, color, 1940, #7	15.00
Brochure, sales, model 14T baler, 24 pp, color, 1958, #8	45.00
Brochure, sales, model 4 mower, 24 pp, black-and-white, 1935, #9	35.00
Brochure, sales, model 4 mower, 24 pp, black-and-white, 1939, #7	28.00
Brochure, sales, model 730 lister, 4 pp, black-and-white, 1930s, #7	8.00
Brochure, sales, model 900 toolbar, 12 pp, black-and-white, 1930s, #9	8.00
Brochure, sales, model A/B tractor, 44 pp, color, 1936, #6	55.00
Brochure, sales, model AR tractor, 19 pp, color, 1951, #8	75.00

Prices

Item	Price
Brochure, sales, model B tractor, introductory brochure, 8 pp, 1935, #9	150.00
Brochure, sales, model B tractor, introductory brochure, model A tractor also, 6 pp, black-and-white, no date (approx. early 1935), #7	150.00
Brochure, sales, model CC cultivator, 24 pp, black-and-white, 1930s, #7	12.00
Brochure, sales, model D tractor, "spoker," 16 pages, color, #6	200.00
Brochure, sales, model D tractor, "spoker," 6 pp w/ foldout poster, color, 1924, #7	250.00
Brochure, sales, model D tractor, authorized distributor announcement, 4 pp, black-and-white, mid-1920s, #6	100.00
Brochure, sales, model G tractor, 8 pp, color, 1948, #6	45.00
Brochure, sales, model GP tractor, 20 pp, black-and-white, 1930, #9	100.00
Brochure, sales, model GP tractor, 32 pp, color, 1930, #8	100.00
Brochure, sales, model MT tractor, 36 pp, color, 1950, #6	55.00
Brochure, sales, model R tractor, 40 pp, color, 1950, #8	125.00
Brochure, sales, models A/B/G/M/MT tractors, 38 pp, color, 1949, #9	100.00
Brochure, sales, models AR/BR/D tractors, 4 pp, color, 1940, #8	35.00
Brochure, sales, Side Delivery Rake, western style, 12 pp, black-and-white, 1930, #7	35.00
Brochure, sales, threshers, 19 pp, black-and-white, 1930s, #8	25.00
Catalog, sales, "Two-cylinder Design" presentation catalog, Models	850.00
Catalog, sales, full line, "Power Farming," 164 pp, 1928, #7	270.00
Catalog, sales, full line, "Power Farming," 78 pp, 1955, #6	55.00
Catalog, sales, full line, "Power Farming," 92 pp, 1956, #7	85.00
Catalog, sales, full line, "Power Farming," 92 pp, 1957, #8	65.00
Catalog, sales, full line, "Power Farming," 96 pp, 1930s, #6	100.00
Catalog, sales, full line, 160 pp, 1920s, #9	250.00
Catalog, sales, full line, master catalog, approx. 800 pp, 1940s imprinted binder, Kansas City branch, #6	500.00
Catalog, sales, General Catalog "5", cloth covered, 264 pp, 1919, #8	350.00
Catalog, sales, General Catalog "6", leather bound, 402 pp, 1928, #8	325.00
Catalog, sales, General Catalog "G", cloth covered, 288 pp, 1920, #7	375.00
Catalog, sales, General Catalog "K", leather bound, 418 pp, 1925, #9	450.00
Catalog, sales, General Catalog, hard bound, 988 pp, 1930s, #8	450.00
Catalog, sales, model D, 16 pp, 1928, #9	75.00
Catalog, sales, models A/B/G tractors, 42 pp, 1938, #7	75.00

Another unbelievable item—a John Deere literature rack in great condition, complete with advertising brochures!

CHAPTER 7

RETAIL PRICE LISTS

R etail price lists differ from sales catalogs by listing the pricing information that is used to actually sell equipment. A sales catalog was basically a listing with pictures of equipment offered for sale by a manufacturer and usually relies heavily on pictures of the equipment being sold. A retail price list was used by the dealer to price the piece of equipment for the farmer.

Price lists often offer little in the way of photographs or illustrations but rely heavily on specifications and all available options for each piece of equipment. A machine is usually listed in a standard configuration with all standard items that are included. Dealer retail price lists are fascinating to read today, as options that are currently either unknown or relatively rare can be found listed as available for order when the machine was new. Retail price lists have resolved many a dispute—and also started a few—as discussions raged over whether a particular piece of machinery left the factory the way it is found today.

Although predating the two-cylinder era, these 1910 retail price lists nicely accent the ones from the 1930s below. Retail price lists are nearly always marked with pencil somewhere, detailing long-forgotten sales deals.

The back of a 1930s price list features great period graphics and logo.

The back of an earlier price list illustrates a Deere warehouse and exhorts the dealer to be wise and buy John Deere goods for long-term quality.

Later price lists at times were enclosed in embossed binders. John Deere's likeness is still there. These small binders were able to be opened and the information updated as necessary.

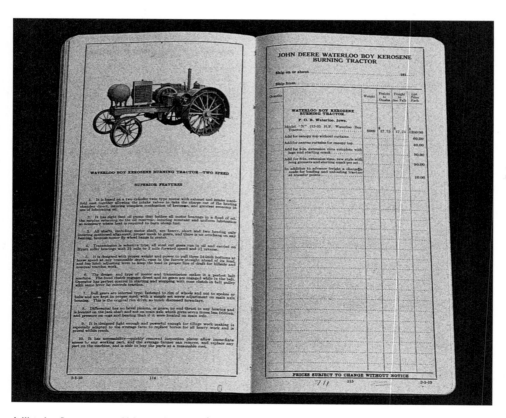

A Waterloo Boy tractor could be purchased for $1,250. That same tractor today, in restored condition, would sell for more than $30,000! If one had only known.

A John Deere plow is shown and pricing information is provided.

The covers of the price lists are often beautifully embossed or imprinted with the company's name, period logos, or even the likeness of John Deere himself! The first few sections of a price list often describe the manner in which equipment is to be ordered, how it is to be shipped, advertising help that is available, and even how the machines are to be paid for by the dealer. It quickly becomes apparent that the retail price lists and the sales catalogs were meant to be used together and complement each other nicely. Many price lists carry the marks and notations of the salesmen who had used them. Quite often, numerous figures can be found written in the margins, and sometimes the prices are even overwritten as price increases were levied. Retail price lists are rapidly increasing in value as collectors realize how important they can be to verify options and variations and the dates they were offered. A set of retail price lists of the two-cylinder tractors from every year, or nearly every year, is quite valuable as an aid in the study of the evolution of Deere's offerings (and of the company itself), both as a collectible and as an aid in restoration. Assembling a set of retail price lists will most likely prove to be very difficult and quite expensive.

Prices

Item	Price
Retail price list, Syracuse, N.Y., 180 pp, black, 1951, embossed binder w/JD's bust, 9.5x5.75 inches, #9	$100.00
Retail price list, Moline, Ill., 120 pp, black, 1947, generic binder, 9.5x6 inches, #6	85.00
Retail price list, Omaha, Neb., 200 pp, black, 1951, printed binder w/JD's bust, 9.5x7.5 inches, #7	125.00
Retail price list, Kansas City, Mo., 237 pp, green, 1941, embossed binder w/JD's bust, 9.5x7.5 inches, #8	125.00
Retail price list and contract, Syracuse, N.Y., 124 pp, orange, 1932, printed softcover, 9x4 inches, #8	85.00
Retail price list and contract, Syracuse, N.Y., 115 pp, green, 1933, printed softcover, 9x4 inches, #8	85.00
Retail price list, Syracuse, N.Y., 164 pp, loose, no binder, 1949, 9x5 inches, #5	50.00
Retail price list, Omaha, Neb., 110 pp, tan, April 1934, printed softcover, 9x5 inches, #6	100.00
Retail price list, Omaha, Neb., 114 pp, green, February 1935, printed softcover, 9x5 inches, #5	75.00
Retail price list, Omaha, Neb., 122 pp, tan, January 1936, printed softcover, 9x5 inches, #7	100.00
Retail price list, Omaha, Neb., 134 pp, green, November 1936, printed softcover, 9x5 inches, #7	85.00
Retail price list, Omaha, Neb., 166 pp, green, January 1937, printed softcover, 9x5 inches, #8	100.00
Retail price list, Omaha, Neb., 176 pp, gray, November 1937, printed softcover, 9x5 inches, #6	85.00
Retail price list, Omaha, Neb., 158 pp, green, October 1938, printed softcover, 9x5 inches, #7	85.00

CHAPTER 8

POSTERS AND DISPLAYS

Posters are, by their very nature, visually oriented and designed to make an impact to convey their message. Posters have been used since early on to advertise machinery, parts, John Deere day, sales, even the dealership itself. Since most posters were printed on paper, nearly all of them have suffered at least a small amount of damage. Posters were, and still are, routinely discarded after their usefulness is finished, which makes a vintage poster in mint condition a rare find today. The most valuable posters feature tractors or a tractor-related theme. The earliest posters were simple exhortations to come to John Deere, try the equipment, and buy it. These were normally predominantly printed words with a small number of photographs or illustrations. Later posters became quite colorful, and the designers spent extra time refining the printed message. Features unique to the Deere machines were called out, as were claims of superior performance and value.

There are a few surviving posters that were originally used by Deere when conducting service schools. These make excellent additions to collections, especially if put to use in a display of vintage tractor parts or toys. While this information is of interest to the collector today, these same facts are often available elsewhere, so the poster's true value is its display value.

Parts such as lynch pins and hardware were sold in displays that increased sales as well as providing a way to organize

Interest in the introduction of a new tractor was drummed up with this poster.

the items being sold. Informational posters and leaflets let the farmer know why John Deere parts were better than the competition. Deere offered specialized displays for items such as batteries, battery cables, fertilizer, oil filters, piston ring sets, light bulbs, spark plugs, and many more items. The displays were primarily constructed of printed cardboard, resulting in

This large poster announces the availability of a rare tractor today, the model 70 standard tread tractor. As usual, the four-legged deer logo is present.

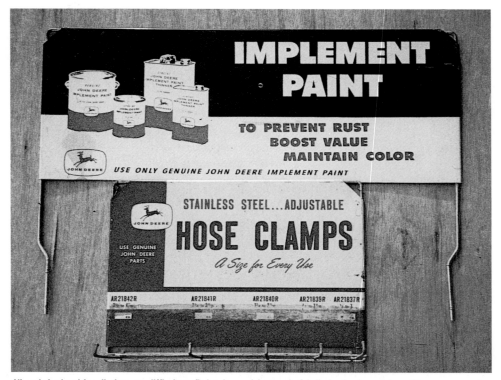

All period advertising displays are difficult to find today, and large colorful display headers such as this one are nearly nonexistent. An added bonus is the depiction of authentic John Deere paint cans. Even everyday items such as hose clamps rated their own special display rack.

This John Deere spark plug display is rarely located in a condition this good. The paper label usually deteriorated and other uses were found for the oak cabinet when it was retired from display duty.

Small clear plastic boxes housed hardware assortments, while the larger clear blue box contained electrical terminals. Although the exact date these were produced is not known, they all feature the four-legged deer logo.

water and handling damage being common. Two-cylinder era displays of any type are rarely seen today and collectors are quick to snap them up as they make a wonderful addition to a vintage exhibit.

Prices

Item	Price
Display, battery cable, metal wall mount w/ part #s, 1960s, #8	$100.00
Display, battery, metal free-standing shelves w/ sign at top, 1950s, #7	250.00
Display, disc blade, cardboard, countertop, leaflets, 1950s, #5	50.00
Display, grease fittings, plastic compartmented box, countertop, 1950s, #8	75.00
Display, hardware, plastic compartmented box, countertop, 1950s, #7	75.00
Display, hitch pin, metal wall mount w/ part #s, 1950s, #7	50.00
Display, hose clamps, metal wall mount w/part #s, 1960s, #8	100.00
Display, JD fertilizers, cardboard, countertop, 6 sample bottles, 1950s, #8	200.00
Display, JD filters, cardboard, countertop, picture of inside of filter, 1940s, #8	100.00
Display, mower guards, cardboard, countertop, leaflets, 1950s, #6	75.00
Display, oil filters, metal free-standing rack w/sign, 1950s, #8	200.00
Display, plowshare, wood free-standing rack w/ 4-legged logo sign on top, 1940s, #7	100.00
Display, pulley brake pad, cardboard, countertop, 1950s, #8	100.00
Display, pump oilers, cardboard, countertop, 1960s, #7	75.00
Display, spark plug, oak case, "John Deere Spark Plugs" wording, #6	200.00
Display, sweeps, cardboard, countertop, w/leaflets, 1950s, #7	75.00
Display, sweeps, metal free-standing rack w/ sign at top, 1950s, #8	100.00
Display, wire cable, metal, free standing, 1950s, #6	50.00
Poster, green w/ white "Coming, John Deere 4-5 Plow Tractor," "See It," "Here August 27th" wording, 38x25 inches, 1954, #9	75.00
Poster, blue w/ white "Syracuse Plows" wording, 6x25 inches, 1930s, #7	30.00
Poster, Field Day Demonstration, 1950s, #6	35.00
Poster, JD Day Invitation, 22x14 inches, 1950s, #4	10.00
Poster, Model 45 combine, 16x18 inches, 1955, #7	40.00
Poster, parts, Genuine John Deere Parts, 24x37 inches, 1940s, #7	50.00
Poster, sales, disc w/picture of model A tractor, 1940s, #6	55.00
Poster, sales, drawn plow, 24x37 inches, 1935, #4	30.00
Poster, sales, manure spreader, 24x37 inches, 1930s, #9	100.00
Poster, service school, Fairbanks Morse RV magneto, 1930s, #7	75.00
Poster, service school, tractor clutch, 1940s, #6	50.00
Poster, service school, tractor PowrTrol hydraulic system, 1940s, #7	50.00
Poster, yellow w/ black "Now On Display–70 Standard Tractor" wording, picture of Model 70 tractor, 38x25 inches, 1954, #9	100.00

CHAPTER 9

PHOTOS, POSTCARDS, AND ADS

Early in Deere's history, the company produced trade cards. These were essentially postcards with advertising printed on them that were mailed or handed out to farmer prospects by salesmen. Certain trade cards are relatively scarce today.

Postcards of Deere's factories are encountered rather frequently, as these were given out to farmers and dealers who

A studio photograph of a new John Deere tractor is flanked by ad slicks for the model 40 tractor and various equipment.

The new model R tractor was shown in all its glory in this studio photograph. Have a question about how your model R looked when it left the factory? Here's your answer!

Official factory advertising was offered to the dealers in kits like these.

attended one of Deere's factory tours. Deere still produces a few postcards today from time to time.

Photographs are another item a collector will run across, ranging from ones that Deere produced to actual photos of life on the farm. Photos of threshing rigs are fairly common and some feature Deere machinery in use. As items like these pass from the ownership of relatives of the people in the photographs, they become available for collectors to add to their collection. Factory or studio photographs are again an invaluable aid to an enthusiast who is attempting to restore his tractor or machine to factory-original condition. These were staged photographs and showed what was usually a production tractor posed for a display picture.

Somewhat difficult to see, these three paper printing blocks were what were shipped to dealers to allow them to place professional equipment ads in local publications. A nice two-page early model D ad serves as background.

The model GP tractor rated a full-page ad in this early trade magazine—the front page, no less! The benefits of the Deere pumping unit and type E engine were easily noticed with this colorful layout on the right.

Ads are another popular form of collectible. It is interesting to follow a machine's evolution through its ads. Changes in horsepower, design, and pricing all occurred as a machine's design changed with the times. Tractors and machines that won awards in regional contests were quick to point out these honors out in new ads. Postcards, photos, and especially ads were all printed on some form of paper and are therefore quite delicate today. It is not uncommon to see ads printed on newsprint literally crumble when they are handled. Special care is advised to preserve and display these fragile items.

Prices

Item	Price
Ad, magazine, Forage Harvester, 5x11 inches, orange/black/white, 1940s, #7	$2.00
Ad, magazine, Model 5 mower, 5x11 inches, orange/black/white, 1940s, #7	3.00
Ad, magazine, Model D & GP tractors, full page, black/white, 1931, #6	5.00
Ad, magazine, Model E engine, full page, black/white, 1930, #8	3.00
Ad, magazine, Power Steering, picture of tractors, full page, color, 1950s, #6	4.00
Ad, magazine, PowrTrol Hydraulics, 8x12 inches, green/black/white, 1946, #7	4.00
Ad, proof, "Genuine John Deere Parts," 4x3 inches, black/white, #10	10.00
Ad, proof, Live hydraulic pump, 6x6 inches, black/white, 1954, #10	10.00
Ad, proof, Model 40 tractor, 6x6 inches, black/white, 1954, #10	12.00
Ad, proof, Model 50/60/70 tractors, 6x6 inches, black/white, 1954, #10	15.00
Ad, proof, Model 60 tractor & Killefer disc, 6x6 inches, black/white, 1954, #10	10.00
Ad, proof, Model L spreader, 2x6 inches, black/white, 1954, #10	10.00
Ad, proof, Model L spreader, 6x6 inches, black/white, 1954, #10	10.00
Ad, proof, Two-cylinder tractor lineup, 6x12 inches, black/white, 1954, #10	15.00
Postcard, "Greetings from Nebraska," picture JD cornpicker, 1960, #6	4.00
Postcard, 30 Series, pics 30 series tractors, 1950s, #8	13.00
Postcard, 4 pics of equipment, "JD Day Invitation," color, 1958, #8	14.00
Postcard, picture of farmer on plow behind horses, 1920s, #6	25.00
Postcard, picture of Harvester Works, color, 1950s, #9	6.00
Postcard, picture of Model 40 tractor & Model 25 combine, color, #9	25.00
Postcard, picture of Model B tractor in hayfield, black/white, 1955, #6	5.00
Postcard, picture of Waterloo Tractor Works, black/white, 1950s, #8	6.00
Postcard, picture of Waterloo Tractor Works, color, 1950s, #9	10.00
Trade card, "Needle In A Haystack," picture JD plow, foldout, early, #7	75.00
Trade card, Deere & Mansur Corn Planters, picture planter, trifold, early, #8	250.00
Trade card, Deere plow, picture, early, #6	120.00
Trade card, Deere plows & cultivators, picture, early, #7	190.00

CHAPTER 10

OPERATION, CARE, AND REPAIR MANUALS

A productive farmer is a happy farmer, and happy farmers buy more equipment. John Deere understood this and wisely sought to keep its customers satisfied with their Deere equipment. Besides offering a selection of quality machinery at a fair price, Deere also understood that the farmer needed to be able to keep his equipment operating. There was a need to develop solid information that could be disseminated among schools and farmers in general. John Deere published a small hardbound book entitled *The Operation, Care, and Repair of Farm Machinery.* Besides offering a needed service, Deere also was able to keep its name in front of many farmers, both new and old. A total of 28 different editions were produced, with the first being published in 1927. The book was originally intended to be used as a teaching aid in high schools

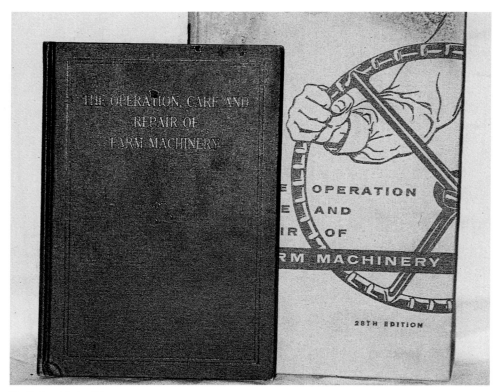

The first and last editions.

An early and later edition of the manuals show the slight difference in cover designs. The typeface on the manual on the right differs, and the decorative logo and printed border are no longer present. The manual in the back illustrates the information to be found inside.

Here they are, a complete set of all 28 editions of the Operation, Care, & Repair manuals. Their value as a textbook is evidenced by the remaining library markings on one of the manuals. Not many collectors can lay claim to owning an entire set.

and colleges, although many farmers found it to be quite handy and thought it should have a place on the farm also. More than 50,000 books were produced that first year, and many were the praises offered up to Deere from those who had received it. The books contained chapters on everything involved in farming, from preparing the seedbed to harvesting the crop to operating the machinery found on the farm. As a new edition was published, Deere updated the machinery and information contained inside as needed. Most of the books averaged around 160 pages or more and Deere placed increasing emphasis on the tractor section as the years passed.

Although 28 editions spanning more than 30 years were published, there were only four basic variations in the covers. The first 22 editions had bluish-gray cloth covers and featured a double-lined printed frame around the edges of the cover. The

next four had plain gray covers with no frame. The 27th edition had a green cloth cover with two bold black bars printed on the cover, while the final (28th) edition was a tan color and presented a tractor steering wheel with the farmer's hand firmly gripping it. All had the edition number printed on the cover, except for the first one, which simply read, *The Operation, Care, and Repair of Farm Machinery.* There was also a Spanish version offered, bringing the total number of editions to 29. By the time Deere finished the 28th edition with its 20 series tractors in it, there were now other teaching aids available from the industry. Today, later editions are quite common and easily found. Earlier versions can still lead a collector on quite a hunt, so study the table below and start your collection

Edition	Year	Edition	Year	Edition	Year	Edition	Year
1st	1927	8th	1934	15th	1941	22nd	1948
2nd	1928	9th	1935	16th	1942	23rd	1950
3rd	1929	10th	1936	17th	1943	24th	1951
4th	1930	11th	1937	18th	1944	25th	1952
5th	1931	12th	1938	19th	1945	26th	1953
6th	1932	13th	1939	20th	1946	27th	1955
7th	1933	14th	1940	21st	1947	28th	1957

Prices

Item	Price
1st, 1927, #9	$300.00
2nd, 1928, #6	150.00
3rd, 1929, #8	70.00
4th, 1930, #7	65.00
5th, 1931, #6	45.00
6th, 1932, #7	45.00
7th, 1933, #4	35.00
8th, 1934, #8	40.00
9th, 1935, #5	35.00
10th, 1936, #6	35.00
11th, 1937, #8	35.00
12th, 1938, #7	35.00
13th, 1939, #6	35.00
14th, 1940, #7	35.00
15th, 1941, #7	30.00
16th, 1942, #8	30.00
17th, 1943, #6	25.00
18th, 1944, #5	25.00
19th, 1945, #8	25.00
20th, 1946, #8	20.00
21st, 1947, #7	20.00
22nd, 1948, #8	17.00
23rd, 1950, #7	17.00
24th, 1951, #6	15.00
25th, 1952, #7	15.00
26th, 1953, #8	15.00
27th, 1955, #9	15.00
28th, 1957, #9	15.00

CHAPTER 11

POCKET LEDGERS
AND
FARM ACCOUNT BOOKS

Perhaps one of the most commonly found paper relics in this hobby is the John Deere pocket ledger. This handy little shirt pocket-sized notebook was designed to be an aid to the farmer. Containing handy measurement, seed, and other charts, it also had numerous blank pages designed for easy record keeping. First published in 1867, the pocket ledger was intended to be a free giveaway that dealers could offer their customers. In return, the dealer's name was prominently displayed on the front of the book, where it would likely be noticed every time the ledger was removed from the farmer's pocket. John Deere benefited by packing multiple machinery ads inside the front and back of the ledger. The name John Deere and the current logo were displayed on the front cover above the dealer's imprint. The back cover usually featured a convenient calendar.

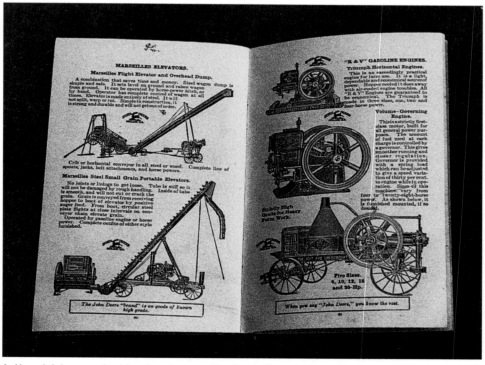

Inside each ledger was advertising of nearly any machine that the farmer might possibly need. Interesting reading today!

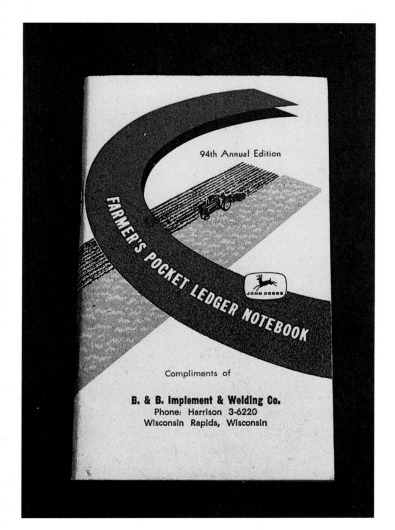

By 1960, when the 94th edition was published, the entire look of the ledger had changed.

Of course, the design of the ledger changed considerably over the years. The earliest ledgers are some of the most striking, as they bear elaborate artwork of both the logo and some of the machinery. As time passed, a more standardized form settled in and remained relatively unchanged until the end of the two-cylinder tractors. Early ledgers were about 40 pages while the later models were around 72 pages. While a pristine ledger is always welcomed, one of the most interesting things about a vintage ledger is the entries that farmers sometimes made in it. Of course, the use of the ledger again affects the condition in which we find them today. Rain, sun, oil, mice, and just plain wear have certainly ruined more than a few ledgers, and price is reflected accordingly. One note: the earliest ledgers, pre-1920, will likely command prices ranging from $100 to more than $400 for the rarest ones, with exceptions going even higher. Not bad for an item that cost dealers around three cents in the mid-1930s!

During this same period, Deere also produced what was known as the *Handy Farm Account Book*. Larger in format, about 8x10 inches and 30 pages, this account book more closely resembled a normal business ledger and was designed to afford a much greater depth of record keeping than the pocket-sized ledger could ever sustain. *The Handy Farm Account Book* also has variations in covers, with the earlier ones

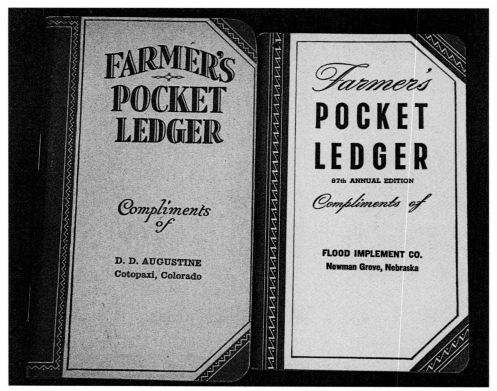

A close-up view of two ledgers reveals that the one on the left is in mint condition and is from a dealer in Colorado, while the one on the right is a 1953 edition from Flood Implement in Nebraska. Both dealerships are long gone. Interestingly, the last items from Flood Implement were just recently auctioned.

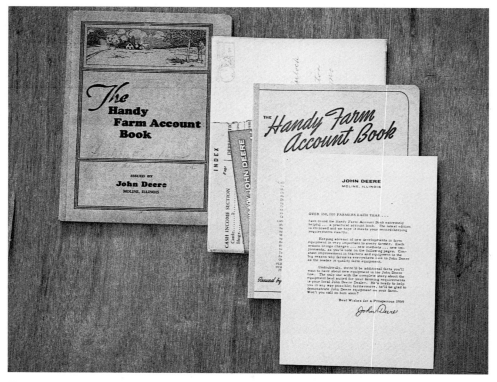

The Handy Farm Account Books are usually not found in this condition. The book on the right still boasts its original envelope and cover letter from Deere.

The very early ledgers are show stoppers and rightly so. They certainly are as expensive as they look. Early examples such as these are exceedingly difficult to locate today. *Bob Key*

Pictured is a nice assortment of the various pocket ledgers that were given away during years past by John Deere dealers. Note the variations in the design and color, with the oldest ledger in the foreground being the most interesting. Most have dealers' names printed on the front, and ledgers have come from as far apart as California and Wisconsin!

being quite ornate. Collectors should also bear in mind that Deere continues producing the pocket ledger to this very day, although it is no longer a common item for Deere dealers to order. Ledgers from the 1980s and 1990s will doubtless turn out to be difficult to locate in years to come. Persistence should pay off, though, and the current difficulty in locating them may translate to future collectibility.

Prices

Item	Price
Ledger, 1923, 57th edition, #6	$115.00
Ledger, 1924, 58th edition, #8	165.00
Ledger, 1925, 59th edition, #5	55.00
Ledger, 1926, 60th edition, #7	135.00
Ledger, 1927, 61st edition, #3	35.00
Ledger, 1928, 62nd edition, #9	95.00
Ledger, 1929, 63rd edition, #8	60.00
Ledger, 1930, 64th edition, #6	25.00
Ledger, 1931, 65th edition, #7	25.00
Ledger, 1932, 66th edition, #6	30.00
Ledger, 1933, 67th edition, #8	15.00
Ledger, 1934, 68th edition, #8	45.00
Ledger, 1935, 69th edition, #7	32.00
Ledger, 1936, 70th edition, #4	15.00
Ledger, 1937, 71st edition, Deere's Centennial year, #7	18.00
Ledger, 1938, 72nd edition, #6	10.00
Ledger, 1939, 73rd edition, #8	26.00
Ledger, 1940, 74th edition, #7	16.00
Ledger, 1941, 75th edition, #7	18.00
Ledger, 1942, 76th edition, #9	20.00
Ledger, 1943, 77th edition, #3	5.00
Ledger, 1944, 78th edition, #6	10.00
Ledger, 1945, 79th edition, #6	10.00
Ledger, 1946, 80th edition, #8	12.00
Ledger, 1947, 81st edition, #8	15.00
Ledger, 1948, 82nd edition, #7	10.00
Ledger, 1949, 83rd edition, #7	12.00
Ledger, 1950, 84th edition, #6	10.00
Ledger, 1951, 85th edition, #9	12.00
Ledger, 1952, 86th edition, #9	18.00
Ledger, 1953, 87th edition, #7	10.00
Ledger, 1954, 88th edition, #7	16.00
Ledger, 1955, 89th edition, #8	10.00
Ledger, 1956, 90th edition, #5	10.00
Ledger, 1957, 91st edition, #7	10.00
Ledger, 1958, 92nd edition, #6	5.00
Ledger, 1959, 93rd edition, #7	8.00
Ledger, 1960, 94th edition, #8	8.00
Book, Handy Farm Account, 1930, #8	15.00
Book, Handy Farm Account, 1939, #5	9.00
Book, Handy Farm Account, 1941, #9	14.00
Book, Handy Farm Account, 1942, #7	14.00
Book, Handy Farm Account, 1950, #9	16.00
Book, Handy Farm Account, 1943, #7	14.00

CHAPTER 12

LETTERHEAD, CONTRACTS, AND INVOICES

J ohn Deere dealers, past and present, were not without their share of paperwork. The overwhelming majority of company-to-dealer interaction, though, was accomplished with letters. Collectors today are able to reap the rewards of all this correspondence by collecting surviving letters and communiqués. These letters, important announcements, and invoices were all printed on letters that had some of the most beautiful letterheads ever seen. Intricate flowing designs were used by Deere on its company letterhead and—again, lucky for the collector—the designs were changed often and varied from branch to branch and factory to factory.

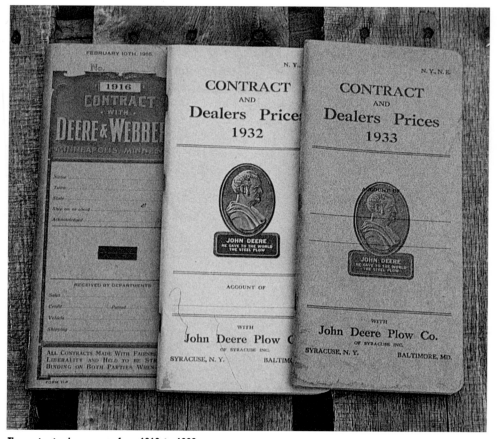

The contracts shown range from 1916 to 1933.

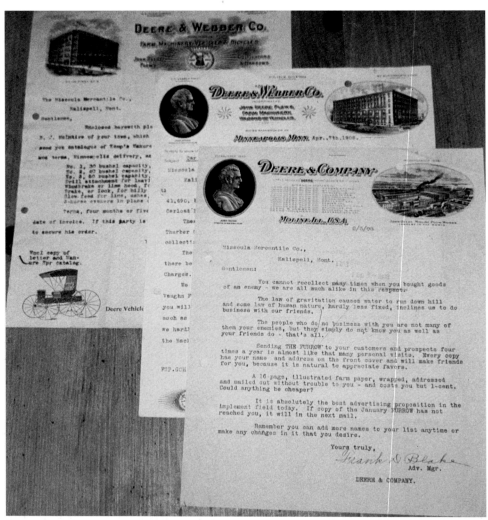

The intricate designs of a few of the different Deere logos are literally works of art. Pictures of the various factories and/or branch houses were present, as was the subtle plug for Deere buggies on the left-most letterhead.

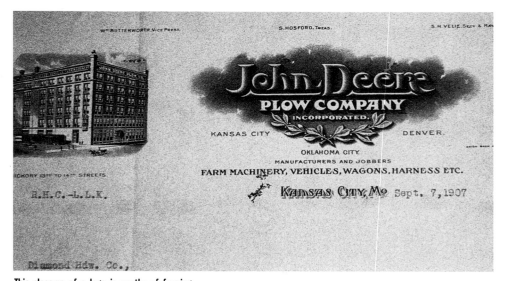

This close-up of a logo is worthy of framing.

Imagine being able to order Waterloo Boy and model D and GP tractors just one more time! These dealer contracts and order forms are seldom, if ever, seen. Looking inside, you can see that the dealer had ordered two new Waterloo Boy tractors!

Every part or machine that was purchased by a dealer would have had a corresponding invoice for the cost mailed to that dealer for his records and payment. These mailings would also feature letters with interesting letterheads. Letters and invoices were usually dated, which makes the job of dating the letterhead style much easier. Most correspondence is fairly routine, although a few letters from Deere were efforts to seek payment or to locate a customer or machine. Some documents also featured advertising for machinery emblazoned on the letter itself, no doubt in an effort not to waste a potential opportunity to gain additional exposure. Many letterheads exhibited pictures of the appropriate branch house and its address.

Dealer contracts— the actual agreement signed between John Deere and the dealer—are a less commonly encountered item. As one would suspect, the rules for doing business with

Dealer stationery and envelopes were not always strictly functional as these colorful examples attest to. Even at the time, it would most surely have seemed almost a crime to dispose of beautiful artwork like this. Today we are glad that some opted to keep it for later generations to enjoy.

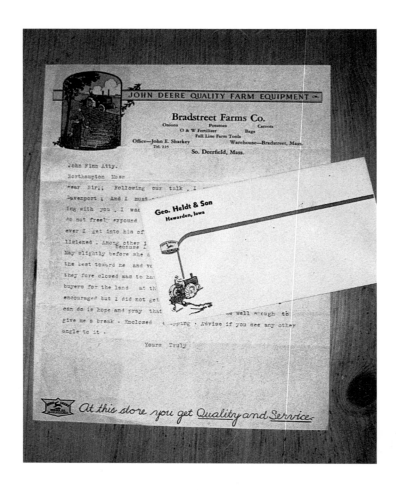

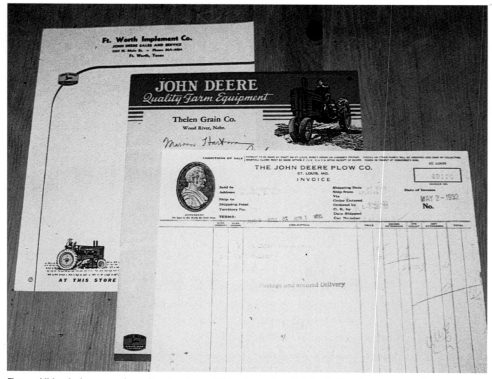

These additional pieces are also quite attractive and John Deere himself is back, this time gracing an invoice copy.

Deere are delineated inside, along with an abundance of legal terminology. Dealer discounts, terms of payment, methods of recourse, freight rates, advertising, and further guidelines from Deere were all listed and both the dealer and a Deere representative signed the contract.

One has to wonder: If society is able to approach the goal of a "paperless" world, what will there be for future generations of collectors and historians to study and collect?

Prices

Item	Price
Contract, dealer's, Calif. branch, equipment pics, order form, 110 pp, 1934, #8	$50.00
Contract, dealer's, Neb. branch, Model D/GP tractors order form 40 pp, 1931, #9	150.00
Contract, dealer's, NE branch, Waterloo Boy order form, 52 pp, 1918, #8	250.00
Envelope, white w/ yellow/green stripe, 4-legged shield logo, "At This Store You Get Quality & Service" wording on back, #7	6.00
Envelope, white w/ color picture of little girl and Model D tractor on steel, picture on back, 1920s, #8	45.00
Envelope, white w/ multi-colored deer leaping over the log logo and pics of various implements on front and back, postmarked 1947, #7	50.00
Invoice, John Deere Plow Co., for new Model A tractor, SN#528617, green paper, October 18, 1943, #9	50.00
Invoice, John Deere Plow Co., parts, green paper, November 13, 1913, #7	10.00
Letterhead, Deere & Company, Moline, Ill., picture of Moline plow works and likeness of John Deere, tan paper, February 3, 1908, #8	25.00
Letterhead, Deere & Webber Co., Minneapolis, Minn., picture of branch building and likeness of John Deere, tan paper, April 7, 1908, #8	25.00
Letterhead, Deere & Webber Co., Minneapolis, Minn., picture of branch building and "sunburst" Deere logo, September 1, 1902, #9	30.00
Letterhead, John Deere Plow Co, Kansas City, Mo., picture of branch building, tan paper, September 7, 1907, #8	25.00
Letterhead, John Deere Plow Co, Portland, Ore., picture of branch building, green paper, March 11, 1905, #8	25.00
Letterhead, John Deere Plow Co., Kansas City & Denver, picture of branch building and "D"/deer head logo, tan paper, March 2, 1898, #6	10.00
Letterhead, John Deere Plow Co., Kansas City, Mo., "Farm Machinery, Vehicles, Wagons, Automobiles, Etc." wording, 1913, #6	10.00

This 1943 invoice was for a new model A tractor, an item in scarce supply during the war. The tractor cost $931.76. Actual tractor invoices are well worth collecting. Because serial numbers are often listed on the invoices, they can be an excellent companion piece to the actual tractor for today's collector.

For many years Deere dealers have been giving away calendars, and the vintage ones that still exist today are valuable collectibles. The determining factors of a calendar's value are the condition, the year, and the pictures on it. Anything that is of two-cylinder-era vintage or older is valuable, and equipment-related pictures are worth more than those with a scenic view. Even modern calendars are worth picking up with an eye to the future, as every year the new John Deere calendar is highly anticipated.

Like a calendar, a thermometer was a practical, useful item to have. It didn't matter if it happened to also have a large John Deere logo and the local dealer's name on it, the price was usually right . . . free! How well it has survived the weather plays a big part in the value of a vintage thermometer. Excessive rust, paint loss, damaged glass, and excessive mounting problems can decimate a thermometer's value. Most Deere thermometers were yellow and had the four-legged logo

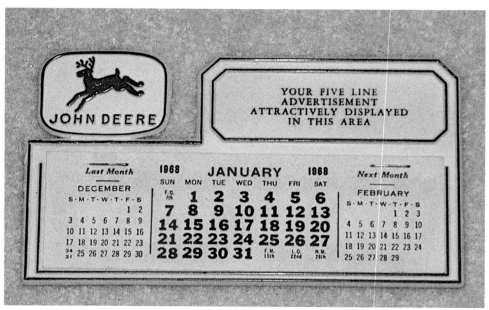

The date is a little late for this book, but the calendar does have the four-legged logo and is indicative of what was available for the dealers to order. *Dave Morrison*

Although well worn, this thermometer is still colorful and the John Deere tractor is easily recognizable.
Melvin and Annette Warren

somewhere on the body. The overwhelming choice for material in a thermometer was metal. A few were made of wood but most of these have not survived nearly so well as the metal thermometers. Quite a few also incorporated a mirror background with some type of picture in front. Still others used a silhouette or shadow box as a thermometer. In addition, there were various specialty thermometers. This variety can make a thermometer collection quite interesting.

Deere also produced several styles of advertising mirrors. Many dealt with a deer or wildlife theme and are a great addition to a display.

The granddaddy of all Deere magazines is *The Furrow*. Published for more than 100 years, it continues to be of great importance to this day. *The Furrow* was mailed to a dealer's customers at the dealer's expense. Although heavy

The left-most magazine is dated 1937 and offers the reader a glimpse at John Deere himself and the fact that it was 100 years ago that he began the company that bears his name. The other issues reflect various themes and cover art.

with Deere advertising, it also featured timely and informative articles on farm-related topics. The paper that *The Furrow* was printed on deteriorates with age, however, and it is getting harder to locate copies in good condition, especially of earlier editions. Special editions, such as Deere's 1937 Centennial issue, seem to bring a better price, as do any early copies. Collectors who have managed to gather up the entire set of *The Furrow* are rewarded with a complete company history!

Prices

Item	Price
Calendar, silhouette, picture of boy w/fishing pole & dog over mountain background, dealer name, 8x10 inches, 1951, #7	$35.00
Calendar, wall, complete, Hinton painting, 10x16 inches, 1944, #7	60.00
Calendar, wall, complete, John Deere Centennial, paintings of John Deere at work on each page, pics of Deere factories, incomplete, #5	20.00
Calendar, wall, complete, picture of famous painting on each page w/ picture of Deere equipment at bottom, four-legged logo, dealer name, 1953, #8	15.00
Calendar, wall, complete, picture of painting, dealer name, Deere advertising, 3.75x5.5 inches, 1892, #8	75.00
Calendar, wall, complete, pics of landscape, four-legged logo, dealer name, 8.75x13 inches, 1958, #7	15.00
Calendar, wall, complete, pics of landscape, four-legged logo, dealer name, NOS, 1960, #10	20.00
Calendar, wall, John Deere & DeLaval, complete, pics of DeLaval equipment, dealer name, unusual, 15x9 inches, 1954, #8	15.00
The Furrow, December—January 1943, #8	15.00
The Furrow, May—June 1949, #7	10.00
The Furrow, May—June, 1943, #7	10.00
Mirror, picture of Model A tractor, four-legged logo w/ dealer name, #8	110.00
Mirror, picture of praying girl w/ four-legged shield logo/dealer name, 5x7 inches, #7	35.00
Mirror, picture of two deer emerging from stream w/ "To Our Dear Friends" wording, dealer name, 9x8 inches, #7	45.00
Thermometer, mirror, picture of "Lucky Horseshoe" has 1951 penny mounted in it, "I Bring Good Luck" "You Will Never Be Broke" wording, four-legged logo, dealer name, 12x5.5 inches, 1951, #8	100.00
Thermometer, mirror, picture of Model A tractor, four-legged logo, dealer name, 1940s, #8	50.00
Thermometer, mirror, picture of Model A tractor, four-legged logo, dealer name, 1940s, #9	75.00
Thermometer, novelty, black, shaped like frying pan, "John Deere" wording, dealer name, 1950s, #8	20.00
Thermometer, shadow box, picture of church, four-legged logo, dealer name, 6x4.5 inches, 1950s, #8	75.00
Thermometer, wall, metal, picture of Model A tractor w/ "John Deere Implements and Trucks" wording, dealer name, 13.25x3.75 inches, #5	65.00
Thermometer, wall, metal, yellow w/ green four-legged shield deer logo, dealer name, 1950s, #8	75.00
Thermometer, wall, metal, yellow w/ picture of Model A tractor, dealer name, irregular shape, 1940s, #8	75.00
Thermometer, wall, metal, yellow w/picture of Model A tractor, four-legged logo, dealer name, 13.25 inches tall, 1940s, #7	100.00
Thermometer, wall, plastic, round w/ four-legged logo, dealer name, 1950s, #8	25.00
Thermometer, wall, wooden, yellow w/ "John Deere Quality Farm Equipment" wording, #10	150.00
Thermometer, wall, wooden, yellow w/"Caterpillar-John Deere-Killefer" wording, 15 inches tall, 1940s, #8	85.00

CHAPTER 14

BINDERS
AND
MISCELLANEOUS ITEMS

There is simply too wide a variety of advertising items to be able to place them all in categories. Items such as shipping and parts tags, salesman's hangers, equipment display tags, specialty advertising and printed material, and

Long torn off and discarded from the parts they were attached to, these paper shipping tags have recently begun to catch the collector's eye. The variety is impressive. Dealer decals are a great view of a bygone time, as their design and names of long-gone dealerships evoke the period during which they were used. The final item is a vintage parts label.

Most collectors would admit to its being a bit difficult getting excited about a battery, even a John Deere battery. But the actual dealership battery sales kit? That's another story!

Forget the incredible information contained in the service bulletins; the binder is a great find in itself! The older blue sales manual in the background bears John Deere's likeness and imparts an air of seriousness, while the later green and yellow sales manual in the foreground is much more colorful and cheerful in its appearance.

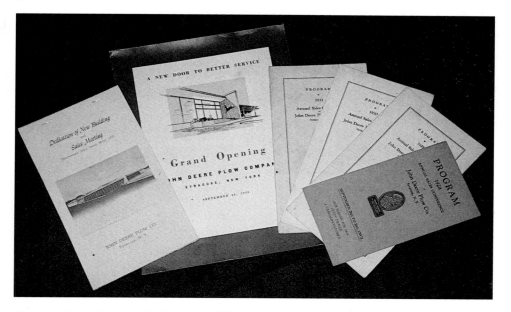

All manner of miscellaneous leaflets have been published by Deere through the years and most are collectible today. Programs from Deere's annual sales conferences of 1928, 1929, 1930, and 1931 are on the right, while the brochures on the left celebrate the opening of John Deere's new Syracuse, New York, parts depot in 1955. It is difficult for us to appreciate the importance of events such as these 50 to 70 years after the fact.

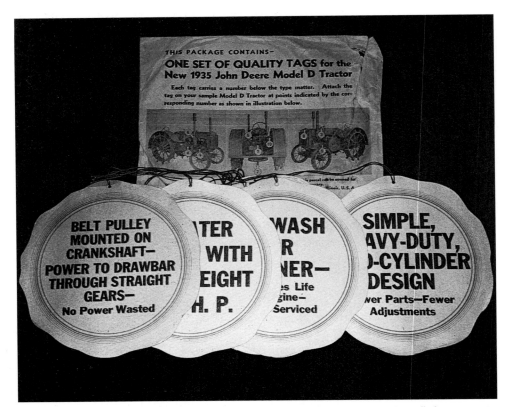

Wow! An unused set of showroom model D feature hang tags. What better way would there be to display an authentically restored 1935 model D tractor than with a set of these?

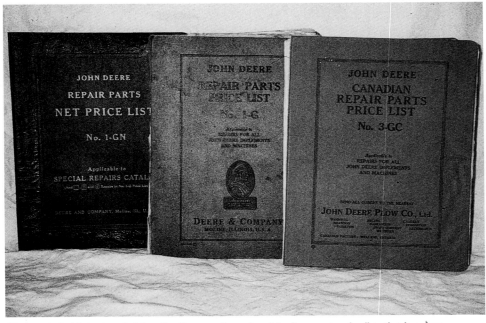

Often overlooked but extremely interesting items are the various John Deere parts price lists that have been published over the years. Some parts change very little in their pricing while others leapfrog skyward in edition after edition. It can also be possible to provide a rough approximation of a date when a part was discontinued and dropped from the price books. The orange Canadian version dates from the time of World War II and inside, wartime price restrictions and exceptions are covered. Fascinating reading.

Specialized parts listings such as these enable collectors to "reverse engineer" parts needs today by studying what was originally available for a piece of equipment and locating an acceptable replacement today. The book in the middle, the "JD Number List," is one of the most overlooked sources of information to be found. Listing all parts that began with the "JD" prefix, it covers bearings and original vendor numbers and John Deere steel and rubber wheels, complete with size specifications. Information like this is very difficult to locate elsewhere.

much more are not easily categorized. Yet these items are far too interesting to simply ignore them and not touch upon them, however briefly. The binders that were supplied with various sales, parts, and service manuals have begun to come into their own as being collectible. These binders were often quite colorful and some featured various embossed designs. Quite a few different binders were made during the two-cylinder era and new ones pop up from time to time. The list that follows exemplifies the types of other printed collectibles that are out there waiting for the lucky collector. Bear in mind that many of these are unknown until discovered and may be one of a kind!

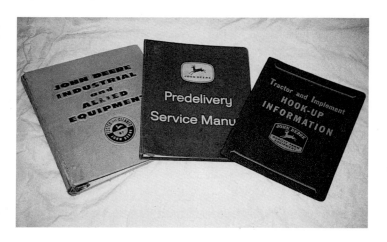

The variety of Deere logos is readily seen in this array of vintage binders. From industrial equipment to predelivery of the equipment to its proper hookup, there was a manual and a special binder for all.

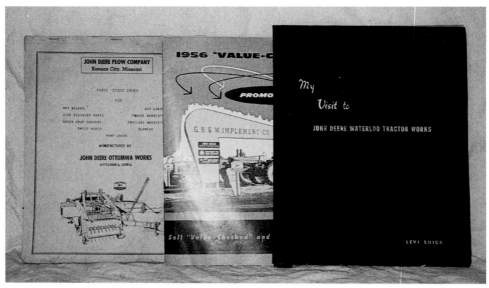

The Ottumwa factory offered dealers the chance to place a stock order for relevant equipment with this handy order form on the left. The year 1956 saw the arrival of Deere's "Valu-Checked" used equipment program that offered a complete standardized package for retailing used machines. The purple velvet-looking book on the right is an example of the souvenir given to attendees of a John Deere Waterloo factory tour. To be found inside was general information and various photographs of tractors and factory scenes. Attendees also found a photograph of their group inside. The attendee's name was printed in gold on the binder. This one formerly belonged to a gentleman named Levi Shick. One wonders what happened to Mr. Shick and his descendants.

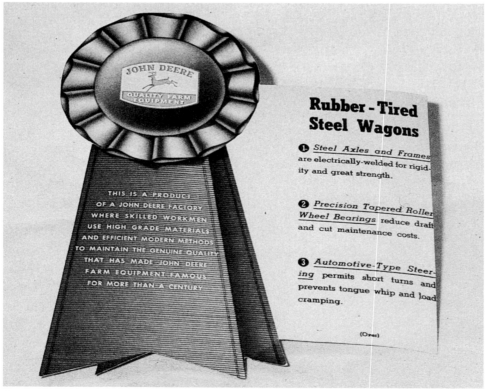

Providing the appearance of a real "winner," these blue-ribbon hang tags were used to point out salient features of John Deere equipment. The blue-ribbon hang tag imparted a subconscious picture in the prospective buyer's mind that John Deere equipment was indeed a "winner!" *Robert Duffel*

Prices

Item	Price
Binder, 4-legged deer logo in white on black background w/ "Flat Rate Manual" wording, 1.25 inches thick 3-ring, #9	$20.00
Binder, Parts, dark green w/ yellow "Parts Catalog" wording and 4-legged logo, #7	30.00
Binder, Price List, dark green w/ yellow "John Deere Price List" wording, embossed likeness of John Deere, #8	50.00
Binder, Sales, dark blue w/gold printing, "John Deere Sales Manual" and likeness of John Deere embossed into cover, #8	40.00
Binder, Service, dark green w/ yellow "Service Manual for John Deere Dealers" wording, #7	35.00
Book, Corny Cornpicker, children's book, 1959, #8	75.00
Book, Johnny Tractor, children's book, 1958, #8	100.00
Booklet, My Visit To The John Deere Factory, purple velvetlike cover, pics of new model A/B/G/H/R tractors, specifications, pics of attending group, factory, etc., #9	100.00
Decal, "John Deere Quality Farm Equipment" "Parts Service" wording in yellow on black background, dealer name, 4.25x2.25 inches, #10	10.00
Hanger, equipment, "Blue Ribbon" w/ sales feature of the model 55 combine, #8	35.00
Hanger, equipment, "Blue Ribbon" w/ sales features of the model 214 baler, #8	35.00
Hanger, salesman's, doorknob, left when farmer was not home, w/ business card, #9	25.00
Hanger, service, w/ suggestions for service, left on tractor steering wheel, #8	25.00
Order Form, John Deere stationery, four-legged logo, samples, 1950s, #9	100.00
Order Form, John Deere uniforms, four-legged logo, 1959, #9	35.00
Pad, order, parts Ottumwa Works, 1950s , #6	15.00
Pad, order, parts, Harvester Works, 1950s , #6	15.00
Receipt, John Deere Plow Co., for payment received on account, "D"/deer head logo w/ "Farm Machinery, Wagons, And Buggies" wording, 3.5x8 inches, blue paper, 1898, #7	8.00
Tag, parts, metal, embossed part number, #8	8.00
Tag, parts, paper, embossed part number, #8	8.00
Tag, parts, yellow paper w/black 4-legged logo, adhesive, #8	2.00
Tag, parts, yellow paper w/black 4-legged logo, black string, #8	3.00
Tag, shipping, "John Deere Farm Implements" wording, 4-legged deer over a log logo, tan paper w/ reinforced eyelet, #6	10.00
Tag, shipping, "John Deere Plow Co. Dallas, TX" wording, tan paper w/reinforced eyelet, #7	10.00
Tag, shipping, "John Deere Plow Co. Moline, ILL" wording, tan paper w/ reinforced eyelet, #7	10.00
Tag, shipping, "John Deere" wording, 4-legged deer logo, yellow w/green printing, reinforced eyelet, #6	10.00
Tags, Model D features & benefits showroom hang tags, #10	200.00
Work Order, four-legged logo w/ dealer name, #8	20.00

John Deere teamed up with the Owatonna Tool Company—
a partnership that continues to this day—and others to provide necessary "special tools" that would be required to perform specific service operations on the two-cylinder tractors. Such items as carburetor service tool kits, diesel injection test benches, injector sleeve pullers, valve-grinding equipment, and many others were all designed by Deere's engineers and made by OTC and others to allow John Deere dealer technicians to more easily complete numerous service operations that might be encountered during the life of a two-cylinder tractor. Many of the wrenches listed in the price guide were originally produced for tractors. They are listed by their original part numbers which are sometimes, but not always, stamped in the wrench. Space does not permit a complete visual guide to all the wrenches and tools listed, so to gain an idea of what each wrench looks like, it is best to study tractor and implement parts catalogs in which early tools were usually listed. Complicating this difficulty in

It is evident from this array of special tool advertising that many different companies developed a wide assortment of tools for John Deere applications. Many names are still familiar today. Indeed, one company in this photograph, OTC, is still Deere's primary specialty tool supplier.

A close-up shows clearly the John Deere name in the top wrench. Difficult to see, the middle wrench is numbered JD-52. The bottom wrench has a cutout name in the handle.

identifying a wrench is that some did not have a part number evident, and others were modified by Deere as the years passed and farmers (or perhaps designers) identified an additional need for this tool that could be addressed by its slight modification. This allowed the same tool to now be used for two jobs instead of one. So it is possible to have two models of the same wrench that are actually different in appearance.

Deere was unable to produce all necessary tools that the two-cylinder tractors required, so the company found it advantageous to research and officially approve tools that might prove helpful to dealers in the servicing of the tractors. These brochures describe the diagnostic tools that Sun and Allen manufactured and Deere approved for use in servicing the two-cylinder tractors.

Prices

Item	Price
Block, Z763H, mower guard & knife repair w/tooling, #6	$150.00
Boring Bar, cylinder, former JD Company tool, #7	2,000.00
Carburetor tool set, JD/OTC dealer's carburetor tool set, #6	200.00
Handle, M2269T, tractor adjustable wheel wrench, #8	15.00
Magnetizer, JD/Allen magneto, #7	400.00
Oil Can, JD60H, blue w/black JOHN DEERE wording, #6	35.00
Oil Can, JD60H, blue w/black JOHN DEERE/dealer name, #7	60.00
Oil Can, JD60H, green w/black JOHN DEERE wording, #5	40.00
Oil Can, JD60H, red w/black JOHN DEERE wording, #5	50.00
Oil can, JD60H, yellow w/black JOHN DEERE wording, #3	25.00
Oil Can, pump, green w/yellow 4-legged logo, #8	35.00
Press, hydraulic crawler track pin/bushing w/tooling, #7	2,000.00
Refacer, JD/Sioux valve w/two-cylinder tooling, #7	250.00
Set, JD/OTC Model M special tool, complete, #8	500.00
Socket, B2296R, tractor spark plug, #8	10.00
Socket, C1591R, tractor head nut, #7	10.00
Socket, F3338R, tractor spark plug, #8	10.00
Socket, H513R, tractor head nut, #7	10.00
Test Bench, JD Diesel injection pump, #7	650.00
Test Bench, JD/Allen magneto, #7	500.00
Wrench set, set of JD 50/51/52/53, #7	50.00
Wrench, A577R, tractor flywheel/lug bolt, #7	70.00
Wrench, AM1023T, tractor steering clutch adjustment, #8	35.00
Wrench, B2297R, tractor flywheel bolt, #7	65.00
Wrench, B353R, tractor flywheel/lug bolt, #7	50.00
Wrench, B353R, tractor flywheel/lug bolt, JD name stamped, #6	65.00
Wrench, B596R, tractor flywheel/lug bolt, #8	55.00
Wrench, D1083R, tractor rod/bearing bolt, #8	65.00
Wrench, D2063R, tractor lug bolt, #7	75.00
Wrench, D2064R, tractor flywheel bolt, #8	110.00
Wrench, Deere & Mansur, #6	35.00
Wrench, H512R, tractor head/flywheel bolt, #9	145.00
Wrench, JD 53, flat steel open-end, #8	10.00
Wrench, JD50, flat steel open-end, #6	10.00
Wrench, JD51, flat steel open-end, #7	10.00
Wrench, JD52, flat steel open-end, #7	10.00
Wrench, JD5C, flat steel, open-end, #5	8.00
Wrench, M2270T, tractor adjustable wheel body, #8	75.00
Wrench, M2278T, tractor wheel, #7	55.00
Wrench, M3420T, tractor adjustable wheel wrench, #7	45.00
Wrench, marked JOHN DEERE both sides, flat steel, #7	10.00
Wrench, S2793D, tractor wheel, #8	65.00
Wrench, w/ words JOHN DEERE cutout in wrench body, #7	50.00

CHAPTER 16

BOXES, SACKS, CANS, AND CONTAINERS

It is perhaps understandable why enthusiasts would want to add parts boxes and containers to their collections. Many of the earlier parts boxes are quite colorful and they came in all shapes and sizes. Early examples were rather plain, being predominantly bare black cardboard boxes with a nice ivory and green parts label applied to the box to identify its contents.

Unfortunately, the cardboard used in these boxes has not weathered the intervening generations very well and most are either damaged or quite brittle today. The next series of packaging bore the familiar green and yellow color scheme, and were the ones most identified with the years the two-cylinder tractors were made. Occasionally, pristine parts boxes are discovered inside other boxes, where they have been protected from

The black box with the ivory label on the bottom dates from the 1920s–1930s while the smaller green and yellow box on top was a familiar sight in dealers' parts departments well into the 1970s while existing stocks were exhausted. Today, one rarely encounters even a green and yellow parts box.

Vintage John Deere paint is hard to find today, as most cans of paint were either used or discarded when the paint was old.

the elements. These boxes are quite vivid in color and are a prized acquisition for a collector. Delco-Remy, Eisemann, Wico, and others all shipped their Deere machine parts in sometimes striking boxes. Additionally, Deere also packaged early paint, oil, and other items in distinctive, 4-legged logo branded cans. Cans, being metal and filled with items that were meant to be used, have not usually survived in good shape to this day. Another area to be considered is that when parts were purchased from the dealer, they were usually placed in bags for the customer to carry them home in. Of course, paper sacks were somewhat flimsy and were usually thrown away. Once again, artwork has changed many times and these parts bags are a neat addition to come across today. All of these factors make parts boxes, cans, and sacks of interest to collectors today.

Packaging has taken various forms over the years. Ranging from the early black to the later green and yellow boxes, a part can be easily dated if one is familiar with the evolution of Deere parts packaging. Metal cans and containers bore attractive graphics, as did parts bags. And always, the John Deere name was present. The only exception was the non-Deere parts that Deere supplied, such as this Wico ignition part in a bright blue box.

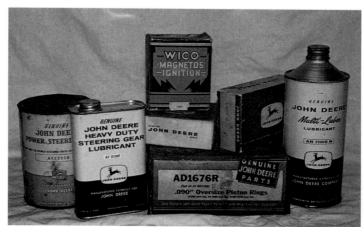

Prices *(note: all containers empty unless otherwise specified)*

Item	Price
Bag, parts, cloth w/black stenciled 4-legged logo, small, #7	$3.00
Bag, parts, cloth w/tag attached, black wording, small, #5	2.00
Bag, parts, gunny sack w/black stenciled 4-legged logo, large, #6	8.00
Bag, parts, tan w/black stenciled Deere & Mansur, small, #7	4.00
Box, black w/ivory label, AC457R tractor part, large, #9	8.00
Box, black w/ivory label, rivets, small, #7	2.00
Box, Eisemann, orange w/lightning bolts, tractor part, small, #8	5.00
Box, orange/black, Delco Remy, tractor part, small, #8	2.00
Box, tan w/green 4-legged logo imprint, tractor part, medium, #7	8.00
Box, tan w/green printing, combine part, medium, #8	6.00
Box, tan w/ivory label, AA952R, tractor part, medium, #9	12.00
Box, tan w/wooden base, yellow label, tractor cylinder block, #7	10.00
Box, tan w/yellow tag, tractor piston kit, medium, #7	8.00
Box, white/yellow/black, tractor decal kit, small, #8	3.00
Box, white/yellow/black, tractor part, large, #8	3.00
Box, white/yellow/black, tractor part, small, #8	2.00
Box, Wico, blue, tractor part, small, #7	3.00
Box, wooden, tractor part, large, #7	10.00
Box, yellow/black, 4 pack tractor oil filter w/carrying handle, medium., #8	10.00
Box, yellow/black, 4 pack tractor oil filter w/carrying handle, Spanish, medium., #7	15.00
Box, yellow/green, AA2052R, tractor part, medium, #10	15.00
Box, yellow/green, toy spreader, small, #8	50.00
Box, yellow/green, toy tractor, small, #6	100.00
Can, orange/black, Delco Remy tractor part, armature, medium., #8	5.00
Can, orange/black, Delco Remy tractor part, field coils, small, #8	4.00
Can, red/black, Fairbanks Morse tractor part, small, #8	4.00
Can, red/black. Fairbanks Morse tractor part, large, #9	8.00
Can, round, quart paint, yellow w/black wording/logo, #7	8.00
Can, round, quart power steering fluid, yellow/green wording/logo, #9	10.00
Can, round, spray paint, yellow w/black wording/logo, #8	10.00
Can, square, hydraulic oil, yellow w/black wording/logo, large, #6	10.00
Can, square, radiator sealer, yellow w/black wording/logo, medium, #6	5.00
Can, square, steering lube, yellow w/black wording/logo, medium, #8	10.00
Crate, wooden pallet, 4-legged logo, #8	30.00
Crate, wooden, AB246R tractor crankshaft, large, #7	25.00
Crate, wooden, B1308R tractor cylinder block, large, #7	20.00
Crate, wooden, combine part, medium, #7	8.00
Crate, wooden, D1343R tractor radiator, large, #7	15.00
Crate, wooden, tractor connecting rod, medium, #7	10.00
Crate, wooden, tractor transmission case, large, #7	20.00
Package, parts, "wax paper," w/black wording/logo and part, medium, #8	3.00
Package, parts, "wax paper," w/black wording/logo, small, #8	1.00
Package, parts, cellophane, w/yellow wording/logo, small, #7	1.00
Package, parts, paper, yellow/green w/ 4-legged logo, small, #10	2.00
Package, parts, paper, yellow/green w/ 4-legged logo, very large, #7	4.00
Package, parts, plastic bubble, yellow w/black wording/logo and part, #9	8.00
Package, parts, plastic, w/black wording/logo, medium, #7	2.00
Sack, parts, tan w/green 4-legged logo and wording, large, #10	8.00
Sack, parts, tan w/green 4-legged logo and wording, small, #10	5.00
Sack, parts, tan w/green wording, medium, #8	6.00
Sack, parts, yellow w/green 4-legged logo and wording, medium, #9	6.00
Sack, parts, yellow w/green 4-legged logo and wording, small, #9	5.00

CHAPTER 17

TIRE PUMPS

There have been several variations in the pump over the years and advanced collectors attempt to collect all of them, although several variants are so scarce as to be almost nonexistent. Early tire pumps had "JOHN DEERE" cast into the main body while the majority simply had a casting number. As they were designed to be used on the power shaft (PTO) of a tractor, the pumps had a female splined coupling to enable them to engage the male PTO of the tractor. Collectors should pay attention to the overall condition of the pump, the chain, and the hose, and the size and variations on the coupling shafts and the method of mounting the shaft to the tractor.

Prices

Item	Price
Pump, 1,000 rpm coupling, rusty, no chain or hose, #5	$100.00
Pump, 1,000 rpm coupling, rusty, original chain, no hose, #5	135.00
Pump, 1,000 rpm coupling, original chain & hose, #8	225.00
Pump, Model L tractor mounting, original hose & chain, #8	450.00
Pump, flywheel mounting, original hose & chain, #8	375.00
Manual, tire pump, original, #8	25.00
Hose, tire pump, New In Box w/gauge, #10	175.00
Fitting, air hose, brass New In Box, #10	40.00
Pump, 1 1/8 540 rpm coupling, rusty, no hose or chain, #4	50.00
Pump, 1 1/8 540 rpm, original chain & hose, #8	100.00
Pump, 1 1/8 540 rpm coupling, rusty, original chain, #6	65.00
Pump, 1 1/8 540 rpm coupling, original hose w/gauge & chain, #9	185.00
Pump, 1 1/8 540 rpm coupling, rusty, stuck, no hose or chain, #3	35.00
Pump, 1 3/8 540 rpm coupling, rusty, no hose or chain, #4	60.00
Pump, 1 3/8 540 rpm coupling, rusty, original hose, no chain, #4	65.00
Pump, 1 3/8 540 rpm coupling, original hose/chain/manual, #9	175.00
Pump, 1 3/8 540 rpm coupling, original chain/manual, no hose, #7	100.00
Pump, 1 3/8 540 rpm coupling, New In Box, w/manual, #10	500.00

CHAPTER 18
SEATS
AND
CASTINGS

Although this book does not attempt to cover the actual two-cylinder tractors and equipment that Deere made, there is one facet of the machines that is worth investigating closer. Deere was fond of casting its name in many different parts that it made through the years. This self-branding placed the Deere name yet again in front of the farmer customer and allowed ready identification of a John Deere-built machine. Sometimes Deere cast the entire John Deere name in a large casting, but most commonly the Deere four-legged logo or "JD" logo was cast into the piece. The comparative scarcity of the actual John Deere name being cast into a piece of iron has led to its collectibility. John Deere has also manufactured many different seats over the years for the operator to sit on while operating the machine in the field. The earliest and most collectible seats were cast iron and some were rather ornate. Deere did not make a large number of cast-iron seats, and all are considered very scarce and desirable today. The cast-iron seat was replaced by stamped steel seats in later years, and as the availability of these seats dwindled and the demand rose, even these later steel seats became sought after. The chances of locating an NOS steel seat of any variety is very

An increasingly popular casting to collect is spare tractor radiator top tanks. The John Deere name is attractively cast into the face of the tank and when painted it is an eye-catching addition to a collection. This tank is from a 1927 model D tractor.

The earliest production tractor seats were made of pressed steel and had over twenty holes. Nearly flat in cross-section, tractors such as the unstyled A, unstyled B, GP, and others used this seat.

slim today, as most that existed have been used in restorations. That makes the few surviving NOS seats highly valuable. Collectors can keep a knowledgeable eye out for nearly any part that has the John Deere name and/or logo cast into it. (A word to the wise: While John Deere was busy making steel seats, so was every other manufacturer in the country. It can be difficult to correctly identify a John Deere steel seat, so it is best to err on the side of caution.)

The tractor seat changed yet again and now only three holes were present. From here Deere would adopt cushioned seats for later models of tractors, as the pressed steel seat was phased out of use.

The next seat to be used was still pressed steel, but now it had a deeper dish to it and the number of holes was reduced to nine.

Prices

Item	Price
Casting, #5 mower gear box lid, "John Deere" wording and 4-legged logo, NOS, #10	$50.00
Casting, A531R, Model A top radiator tank, "John Deere" cast into tank, #8	125.00
Casting, AB241R, Model B front hubcap, "JD" cast into cap, #8	50.00
Casting, AD357R, Model D rear axle hubcap w/drawbolt, "JD" cast into cap, #6	25.00
Casting, B394R, Model B top radiator tank, "John Deere" cast into tank, #7	100.00
Casting, D327R, Model D front hubcap, "JD" cast into cap, #7	20.00
Casting, D53R. Model D top radiator tank, "John Deere" cast into tank, #7	100.00
Casting, F R, Model G top radiator tank, "John Deere" cast into tank, ultra rare "low radiator" top tank, #7	500.00
Casting, iron, planter lid, Y1521B, "Deere & Mansur Company Moline, III" & side view of deer cast into lid, #8	75.00
Casting, iron, planter lid, Y2002B, "Deere & Mansur Company Moline, III" & full frontal view of deer cast into lid, #9	75.00
Casting, iron, plow, M626A, rear axle bracket, "John Deere" cast into bracket, #8	50.00
Casting, iron, trans cover, D5R, "Waterloo Gasoline Engine Company" cast into cover, ultra rare "spoker" D cover, #8	700.00
Casting, JD2200, Model D front hubcap, "JD" cast into cap, NOS, #10	50.00
Casting, Van Brunt grain drill seed box end, "VB" logo cast into end, #8	75.00
Lid, steel, planter, Y4965B, "John Deere Moline, III" embossed into lid, #7	35.00
Plate, steel, planter name plate, Y5028B, "John Deere Planter" embossed into plate, #7	50.00
Seat, iron, implement, "Deere & Co"/"Moline, III" cutout in seat, #9	300.00
Seat, iron, implement, "Deere & Co"/ Moline, III" cutout in seat, broken letters, #6	200.00
Seat, iron, implement, "Deere & Co"/"Moline, III" cutout in seat, #9	500.00
Seat, iron, implement, 36 slot, #9	100.00
Seat, iron, implement, round, "Deere & Mansur Co. Moline, III" cast into seat, ornate cutout designs in seat, #8	300.00
Seat, steel, implement, JD54, "flat" 27 hole, NOS, #10	150.00
Seat, steel, implement, K1102B, 30 slots, #8	65.00
Seat, steel, implement, K1232B, 25 hole, #7	50.00
Seat, steel, tractor, AD1606R, 3-hole seat, #8	75.00
Seat, steel, tractor, AD1606R, 9-hole seat, #8	75.00
Seat, steel, tractor, C1785R, "flat" 24-hole seat, #8	100.00
Seat, steel, tractor, D1786R, 24-hole seat, larger, #8	75.00
Shield, Model 12A combine, "John Deere" & 4-legged deer logo embossed into shield, large, #8	100.00
Tank, top radiator, #3 combine, brass, "John Deere" embossed into tank, #8	75.00

CHAPTER 19

NEW OLD STOCK (NOS) PARTS

Those collectors who collect parts often seek out each variation of a specific part. The evolution of a particular part can then be documented as it changed through the years. An additional bonus to collecting NOS parts is that often instructions were included in the box with the part. This provides irrefutable proof as to exactly how and where a part was to be installed.

The true value of an NOS part is twofold. The first criterion to consider is what exactly the part is. For example, an

An NOS 24-inch spoked flywheel for a "spoker" model D tractor. This flywheel was used on the 1925 model D tractors and the discovery of an NOS flywheel is nearly unbelievable. Deere changed to solid flywheels in 1926, as numerous accidents had occurred in which farmers had managed to get an arm tangled in a spoked flywheel. And so the "spoker" flywheel faded into the beginnings of a legend.

The colors on this John Deere—supplied Wisconsin engine oil filter cannot be described. To an advanced collector, the transition from the relatively plain cardboard box to the jewel found inside can be likened to the discovery of a treasure chest. Although an NOS filter like this would certainly put the finishing touch on a flawless restoration, it is simply too attractive in a display to be considered to be used on an engine.

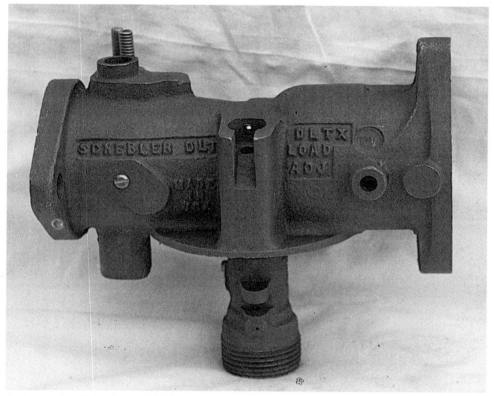

Another once-in-a-lifetime find, an NOS Schebler DLTX51 "big-nut" model G tractor carburetor body. The DLTX51 is nicknamed the "big nut," as the bottom bowl retaining nut is far larger on this model of carburetor than the regular carburetors. This carburetor flowed more fuel to allow the giant model G to develop its impressive increase in horsepower. Collectors and tractor pullers alike value this carburetor highly for its power-making potential.

Another great shot of
this intriguing piece.

NOS hood medallion for an R diesel would be of far greater value than an NOS frame bracket for a cultivator. The second criterion is the part's appearance. Collectors like NOS parts to look new, not neglected. A little dust is acceptable, but large areas of rust are not. Also, if the part was originally packaged, then a pristine package or box is a major benefit. Basically, the part should look like it has been sitting on a dealer's shelf for 60 years, waiting for someone to buy it, not like it had lain out forgotten in the chicken coop. Condition and content are the keywords.

The pricing guide contains a few examples of used parts to highlight the differences between good used parts and NOS parts. Parts are identified primarily by their casting numbers, as many times the part number has been lost or damaged.

Prices

Item	Price
Air Cleaner, AD2816R, Model D tractor, NOS, #10	$200.00
Bearing, connecting rod, AC456R, Model GP tractor, NOS, #10	150.00
Bearing, connecting rod, AD671R, Model D tractor, NOS, #10	150.00
Block, engine, AC257R, Model GP tractor, NOS in crate, #10	1,500.00

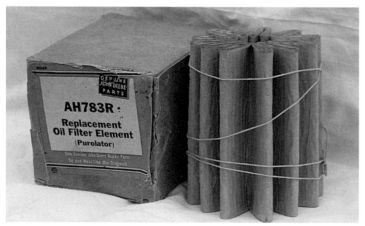

Early two-cylinder tractors were not equipped with engine oil filters. This changed over the years and the earliest filters looked like this example. One can see that it is constructed of paper and so relatively few would have survived to this day. This filter was intended for a model H tractor.

Item	Price
Block, engine, AD391R, Model D tractor, NOS in crate, #10	850.00
Block, engine, F48R, Model G tractor, used, #8	750.00
Block, engine, R48R, Model R tractor, NOS in box, #10	1,000.00
Block, engine, R690R, Model R tractor pony motor, NOS in box, #10	650.00
Core, radiator, AD1383R, Model D tractor, NOS in crate, #10	500.00
Crankshaft, A103R, Model A tractor, NOS in crate, #10	450.00
Crankshaft, B114R/AB246R, Model B tractor, NOS in crate, #10	500.00
Crankshaft, F3560R, Model 730 diesel tractor, NOS in box, #10	1,500.00
Crankshaft, R1303R, Model 830 diesel tractor, NOS in crate, #10	850.00
Crankshaft, R340R, Model R tractor, NOS in crate, #10	750.00
Drawbar, R1318R, Model 830 diesel tractor, NOS, #10	175.00
Fan, engine, AA205R, Model A tractor, rubber hub, NOS, #10	500.00
Fan, engine, AD49R, Model D tractor, friction disc hub, NOS, #10	200.00
Fan, engine, AD49R, Model D tractor, friction disc hub, used, #6	45.00
Flywheel, D33R, Model D "Spoker" tractor, 24 version, 1925, NOS, ultra rare, #10	4,000.00
Generator, AD2738R, Model D tractor, NOS in box, #10	350.00
Grille, AA6300R, Model 60 tractor, NOS in box, #10	500.00
Grille, AM746T, Model M tractor, NOS in box, #10	1,000.00
Grille, RH, AB1534R, Model B tractor, NOS, #10	250.00
Head, cylinder, C1701R, Model GP tractor, 6-inch bore, NOS, #10	1,500.00
Head, cylinder, C250R, Model GP tractor, 5.75-inch bore, NOS, #10	600.00
Head, cylinder, C250R, Model GP tractor, 5.75-inch bore, used, #7	350.00
Head, cylinder, F49R, Model G tractor, NOS, #10	1,800.00
Head, cylinder, F49R, Model G tractor, rebuilt w/valves, #8	750.00
Head, cylinder, R49R, Model R tractor, NOS, #10	1,000.00
Injector, water, AD104R, Model D tractor, NOS, #10	175.00
Jewel, dash, AA4925R, Model 730/830 tractor & more, NOS, #10	75.00
Manifold, A36R, Model A tractor, NOS, #10	300.00
Manifold, B73R, Model B tractor, NOS, #10	300.00
Manifold, D42R, Model D tractor, NOS, #10	350.00
Muffler, AA1778R, Model A tractor, NOS, #10	135.00
Muffler, AR1594R, Model 830 diesel tractor pony motor, NOS, #10	100.00
Pipe, water, A733R, "open fanshaft" early Model A tractor, NOS, #10	2,000.00
Piston, B1R, standard all fuel, Model B tractor, NOS, #10	125.00
Piston, B2725R, .045 o.s., hi-altitude gasoline, Model B tractor, NOS, #10	125.00
Piston, D1172R, .090 o.s., Model D tractor, NOS, #10	250.00
Piston, Model E 1.5 hp engine, NOS, #10	75.00
Piston, R944R, .045 o.s., Model R tractor, NOS, #10	250.00
Pulley, belt, D1706R, Model D tractor, NOS in crate, #10	300.00
Rod, connecting, AD2498R, Model D tractor, NOS in crate, #10	300.00
Rod, connecting, C1922R, Model GP tractor, 6-inch bore, NOS, #10	300.00
Rod, connecting, C1922R, Model GP tractor, 6-inch bore, used, #7	175.00
Rod, connecting, C226R, Model GP tractor, 5.75-inch bore, NOS, #10	300.00
Rod, connecting, R234R, Model R tractor, NOS in crate, #10	350.00
Tank, fuel, AA376R, "center fill," very early Model A tractor, NOS, #10	1,000.00
Tank, fuel, AR1109R, Model 820 diesel tractor, NOS, #10	300.00
Tank, fuel, AR365R, Model R tractor, NOS, #10	300.00
Wheel, steering, AA380R, Model A/G tractor & more, NOS, #10	150.00
Wheel, steering, AM3914T, Model 330/430 tractor, NOS, #10	350.00
Wheel, steering, AR505R, Model R tractor, 4 spoke, NOS, #10	200.00

Just the thing to top off a restoration, the medallion on the left identifies the tractor it is on as being equipped with power steering. The leaping deer cap on the right finished off the center of a tractor steering wheel.

NOS parts have one feature that other parts do not have: They are new. To parts collectors, this is critical. The most valuable parts are the ones that are truly NOS and still retain their original packaging. NOS parts in this picture range from a piston for a model 820 tractor to a new dash panel for a model A tractor to a new main bearing for a model G tractor. NOS parts are never reproductions but real parts, just as they came from Deere.

CHAPTER 20

CARBURETORS, MAGNETOS, AND GAUGES

C arburetors, magnetos, and even gauges are also being added to collections. Although an item like a carburetor is best ultilized on a tractor, the early, brass-bodied carburetors are a nice display item, especially when polished. Styles and brands of magnetos have changed many times throughout the years and certain models are very, very difficult to locate. There are enough different ones to keep serious collectors busy for quite some time. Many times, the carbs and mags have been modified and the necessary parts to restore them are almost impossible to find. Most carburetors used on John Deere equipment were manufactured by the Marvel–Schebler company and a few by the Ensign company.

John Deere itself manufactured only one magneto during the two-cylinder era and this is it. It has been speculated that Deere made this magneto to make the statement to its magneto suppliers that if they did not treat the company honestly, Deere would have no problem producing its own magneto. Another explanation is that Deere had these made for them by the Fairbanks-Morse Company. Whatever the reason, Deere dropped this design and continued to rely on vendor-supplied magnetos. The "John Deere Tractor Co." wording on the body is breathtaking. This magneto originally was installed on certain models of the GP tractor, and as most were replaced long ago, collectors should keep their wallets handy when asking the price on a John Deere magneto!

The most common two-cylinder carburetor is the Marvel-Schebler. Crucial to determining application and value, all carburetors of this design had their model number stamped in this location. The prefix DLTX began every model number. Many is the collector who has discovered that his new purchase has the incorrect carburetor model on it.

The favorite of John Deere and today's collectors is the Wico brand magneto. Its sturdiness, reliability, and the ready availability of parts serve to make the Wico magneto the continuing choice of collectors.

The carburetor shown above is referred to as a "cast iron" Schebler. Early models of tractors were originally equipped with a "brass body" Schebler. Collectors know how difficult it can be to locate an original brass Schebler carburetor.

The most common manufacturers of magnetos were Wico, Fairbanks-Morse, and Edison-Splittdorf. The earliest magnetos were made by Edison-Splittdorf and, as with the carburetors, most parts are simply not available today. Fairbanks-Morse magnetos arrived on the scene early but were phased out after several years in favor of the more reliable, simpler, and less expensive Wico magnetos. The Wico stayed on as standard equipment until the Delco-Remy battery ignition distributor finally replaced the magneto altogether.

Bright and shiny, these magnetos and carburetor are a far cry from their condition when they were removed from a tractor. Bead blasted and rebuilt, they take on a life separate from their intended purpose. Although most are again installed on a machine, some are lovingly laid in a favorite spot where a collector's eye might rest on it from time to time.

This nice assortment of NOS gauges showcases the variety in artwork on the face of the gauges.

The AB2568R ammeter is an example of the sought-after "white-face" gauge. The artwork on this gauge appears almost Frankenstein-like.

The AA1730R oil pressure gauge is also a "white-face" gauge. The red mark on the dial designates the low point on the engine oil pressure and the word "Stop" is also present as an apparent reminder to farmers that if your engine does not have oil pressure, it is time to "stop" the engine. Amazingly, many times little or no attention was paid to this basic warning, with disastrous results.

Original gauges on the letter series two-cylinders and the very first numbered series have come to be known as white-face gauges. The background of the gauge face was white with black printing on it. Replacement gauges today, although available for nearly any two-cylinder tractor, are known as black-face.

The good thing about collecting items like this is that if and when a collector desires to dispose of his collection, he will have no problem at all finding interested buyers. NOS pieces bring premium prices, used pieces bring far less. Keep an eye on the hay wagons at the auction; many times a gauge or magneto or carburetor will surface there.

Prices

Item	Price
Carburetor, AA200R, Model A tractor, brass DLTX8, #8	$250.00
Carburetor, AA200R, Model A tractor, brass DLTX8, NOS in box, #10	850.00
Carburetor, AA3950R, Model A tractor, iron DLTX71, #7	175.00
Carburetor, AA5344R, Model 60 tractor, iron DLTX81, #7	250.00
Carburetor, AB237R, Model B tractor, iron DLTX10, #8	250.00
Carburetor, AB3533R, Model B tractor, iron DLTX67, #7	175.00
Carburetor, AC174R, Model GP tractor, "Ensign" brass, #8	350.00
Carburetor, AD107R, Model D "Spoker" tractor, brass, 1925, #8	500.00
Carburetor, AD2544R, Model D tractor, iron DLTX63, NOS in box, #10	450.00
Carburetor, AF3775R, 4-cylinder pony motor, #7	125.00
Carburetor, AL2848T, Model LA tractor, NOS, #10	300.00
Carburetor, AR850R, 2-cylinder pony motor, #8	125.00
Carburetor, LP, AB5285R, Model 530 tractor, #8	250.00
Distributor, AA4877R, Model A/B/G tractor, NOS in box, #10	250.00
Distributor, AR1370R, 4-cylinder pony motor, NOS, #10	300.00

Item	Price
Distributor, w/drive, LP, AA6041R, Model 50/60 tractor, #8	200.00
Gauge, ammeter, AB2568R, tractor, white-face, NOS in box, #10	75.00
Gauge, ammeter, AM1864T, black-face, #8	35.00
Gauge, ammeter, AM354T, tractor, white-face, #6	35.00
Gauge, ammeter, AM810T, tractor, white-face, NOS in box, #10	150.00
Gauge, fuel, AF2721R, tractor, 12-volt, black-face, NOS in box, #10	200.00
Gauge, fuel, AF2739R, tractor, 6-volt, black-face, NOS in box, #10	200.00
Gauge, oil, AA1730R, tractor white-face, NOS in box, #10	150.00
Gauge, oil, AB1549R, tractor, white-face, NOS in box, #10	150.00
Gauge, oil, AB292R, tractor, white-face, NOS in box, #10	150.00
Gauge, oil, AF2868R, tractor, black-face, NOS in box, #10	150.00
Gauge, oil, AL2811T, tractor, white-face, NOS in box, #10	150.00
Gauge, oil, AL2948T, tractor, white-face, NOS in box, #10	150.00
Gauge, oil, AM737T, tractor, white-face, #8	75.00
Gauge, oil, AR492R, tractor, white-face, NOS in box, #10	150.00
Gauge, temperature, AA3534R, tractor, white-face, #8	75.00
Gauge, temperature, AA6295R, tractor, black-face, #7	75.00
Gauge, temperature, AA6295R, tractor, black-face, NOS in box, #10	150.00
Gauge, temperature, AA952R, tractor, white-face, conversion kit, NOS in box w/directions, #10	200.00
Gauge, temperature, AB3066R, tractor, white-face, #8	75.00
Gauge, temperature, AF2774R, tractor, black-face, NOS in box, #10	150.00
Gauge, thermometer, AD1063R, type W power unit, #7	600.00
Hour meter, AA5338R, Model A tractor, 12-volt, NOS in box, #10	200.00
Hour meter, AB4282R, Model B tractor, 6-volt, #6	50.00
Hour meter, AB4282R, Model B tractor, 6-volt, NOS in box, #10	175.00
Hour meter, AM1660T, Model M tractor, 6-volt, NOS in box, #10	150.00
Hour meter, AR589R, Model R tractor, NOS in box, #10	350.00
Hour meter, AT11369, Model 435 diesel tractor, #9	150.00
Magneto, AA201R, Model A tractor, "Fairbanks-Morse RV," rare, #8	450.00
Magneto, AA3870R, Model A/B/G tractor, #7	150.00
Magneto, AB706R, Model B tractor, "Fairbanks-Morse RV2," #8	400.00
Magneto, AC1176R, Model GP tractor, Fairbanks-Morse, #7	300.00
Magneto, AC432R, Model GP tractor, "John Deere" built, rare, #8	750.00
Magneto, AD597R, Model D tractor, "Edison-Splittdorf," #8	400.00
Magneto, AE36RT, type E engine, #8	250.00
Magneto, AL2908T, Model LA tractor, #7	175.00
Tachometer, AA5745R, Model A/60 tractor, NOS in box, #10	500.00
Tachometer, AB4736R, Model B/50 tractor, #7	100.00
Tachometer, AB4736R, Model B/50 tractor, NOS in box, #10	225.00
Tachometer, AM3492T, Model 420 tractor, NOS in box, #10	500.00

CHAPTER 21

STEEL AND ROUND-SPOKE WHEELS

The round-spoke wheel and, to a lesser degree, the factory flat-spoke wheel are the ultimate rubber tire wheel for antique tractors. Round-spoke wheels gave way to less expensive cast-iron center wheels with demountable rubber tire wheels, and the day of the round-spoke wheels was finished. Obviously there is a finite supply of steel and round-spoke wheels remaining today. Factor in that the wheels varied from one model of tractor to another and the availability of good wheels, both steel and rubber, is a constant problem. The wheels also changed design as the years went by and certain wheels were only original on certain tractors. Implement wheels have not been as big a source of interest for the collector, as most were

Ugly is the word that comes to mind with this rim. Not only is it a cutoff, the model D rim also added insult to injury when concrete was poured in among the spokes for weight! Believe it or not, many is the collector who has patiently removed the very same concrete from wheels such as these in an attempt to better the appearance of the wheel.

Another view of a factory round-spoke wheel, this time a rear wheel.

A model D tractor flat-spoke steel front wheel. Basically the same as the round-spoke steel wheels, the flat-spoke front steel wheels were used essentially in 1929 only on the model D and GP tractors. Breakage was common and the round-spoke wheel was reintroduced. Notice the factory swaging of the spoke to the steel rim. This is crucial in identifying original steel wheels.

Put this one in the "Makes You Want to Cry" file. A factory round-spoke rear rim was sacrificed to convert a steel wheel to a rubber rim. One can only hope the round-spoke rim came from an International Harvester tractor and not a John Deere!

A model A tractor round-spoke steel front wheel. Notice the steel band that replaces the rubber tire. It is important to remember that steel wheels predate rubber tires.

not converted to rubber. Those that were are usually restored in this condition with an eye toward eventually spotting an original implement steel wheel. The scarcity of tractor wheels has prompted most advanced collectors to purchase any wheel they might happen across in their travels. Wheels in excellent condition are setting new pricing records at every auction lucky enough to have such a set. Collectors should bear this in mind when arguing over the price of a pair of wheels!

A model A tractor round-spoke rubber front wheel. The ultimate in rubber tires, the round-spoke wheel continues to rise in value. Note the factory swaging of the spoke to the rim.

The dreaded "cutoff" rubber wheel. Many steel wheels were converted to rubber by having their steel rims cut off and a rubber rim welded to the remnants of the spokes. These are not very desirable today, because many times the damage was compounded when shade tree mechanics further modified the rims with reinforcements of their own design. Note the tabs that have been added to the spokes and where the spoke was welded, not swaged, to the rim.

Prices *(all prices per single wheel)*

Item	Price
Wheel, cast-steel front, AC830R, Model GPO tractor, #8	$1,800.00
Wheel, cast-steel front, AC847R, Model A/GPWT tractor, #8	800.00
Wheel, flat-spoke rear, JD1270, 9.00x36 inches, Model A/B tractor, #8	300.00
Wheel, flat-spoke rear, JD1271, 10.00/11.25x36 inches, Model A/B tractor, #7	300.00
Wheel, round-spoke rear, AC1103R, 9.00x36 inches, Model GPWT, #8	1,000.00
Wheel, round-spoke rear, AD1418R, 12.75/13.50x28 inches, referred to as "12 spline Model D tractor round-spoke rear," #8	600.00
Wheel, round-spoke rear, AD972R, 12.75x28 inches, referred to as "6 spline Model D tractor round-spoke rear," #8	500.00
Wheel, round-spoke rear, AF411R, 10.00x36 inches, referred to as "Model G tractor round-spoke rear," #8	1,500.00
Wheel, round-spoke rear, AF411R, 10.00x36 inches, referred to as "Model G tractor round-spoke rear," rusted holes, cracked hub, #5	600.00
Wheel, round-spoke front, AB378R, 5.00x15 inches, referred to as "Model B tractor round-spoke front," #8	550.00
Wheel, round-spoke front, AC1062R, 6.00x16 inches, Model AR/D/GP tractor, #7	275.00
Wheel, round-spoke front, AC1088R, 5.50x16 inches, referred to as "Model A tractor round-spoke front," #8	500.00
Wheel, round-spoke front, AD990R, 7.50x18 inches, referred to as "Model D tractor round-spoke front," #8	225.00
Wheel, round-spoke rear, AA385R, 9.00x36 inches, referred to as "Model A tractor round spoke rear," #8	500.00
Wheel, round-spoke rear, AB375R, 7.50x36 inches, referred to as "Model B tractor round-spoke rear," #8	500.00
Wheel, round-spoke rear, AC1070R, 11.25x24 inches, Model BR/BO/GP tractor, #7	400.00
Wheel, steel, flat-spoke front, AD536R, Model D tractor, #7	750.00
Wheel, steel, flat-face rear, JD1214, Model A tractor, #7	800.00
Wheel, steel, flat-face rear, JD1215, Model B tractor, #7	800.00
Wheel, steel, flat-face rear, JD1227, Model G tractor, #9	1,500.00
Wheel, steel, front, AA787R, Model AN tractor, #7	1,800.00
Wheel, steel, front, AB358R, Model B tractor, #6	700.00
Wheel, steel, front, AB427R, Model BN tractor, #8	1,800.00
Wheel, steel, front, AB642R, Model BR/BO tractor, #8	1,000.00
Wheel, steel, front, AC439R, Model GP tractor, #7	800.00
Wheel, steel, front, AC885R, Model A tractor, #8	800.00
Wheel, steel, front, AC885R, Model GPWT tractor, #4	500.00
Wheel, steel, front, AC885R, Model GPWT tractor, #9	1,200.00
Wheel, steel, front, AD900R, Model AR/D tractor, #8	500.00
Wheel, steel, front, AF210R, Model G tractor, #9	1,500.00
Wheel, steel, front, JD1279, Model R/80/820/830 tractor, #8	1,800.00
Wheel, steel, rear JD1212, Model GPWT tractor, #7	1,000.00
Wheel, steel, rear, AD38R, "spoker" model D tractor, #8	1,200.00
Wheel, steel, rear, AF1713R, Model 720/730 tractor, #6	1,600.00
Wheel, steel, rear, JD1200, Model D tractor, #7	600.00
Wheel, steel, rear, JD1202, Model GP/GPO tractor, #7	750.00
Wheel, steel, rear, JD1217, Model AR tractor, #7	750.00
Wheel, steel, rear, JD1219, Model D tractor, #8	600.00
Wheel, steel, rear, JD1221, Model BR tractor, #7	850.00
Wheel, steel, rear, JD1280, Model R/80/820/830 tractor, #8	1,600.00
Wheel, steel, reversible rear, AD1389R, Model D tractor, #9	1,200.00
Wheel, steel, skeleton rear, C1547R, Model GPWT tractor, #8	1,500.00
Wheel, steel, skeleton rear, JD1224, Model B tractor, #8	750.00
Wheel, steel, skeleton rear, JD1225, Model A tractor, #8	800.00
Wheel, steel, skeleton rear, JD1228, Model G tractor, #8	1500.00

CHAPTER 22

COMPANY
AND
DEALERSHIP
EMPLOYEE ACCESSORIES

Many items have been produced during the past 80-plus years that were intended for Deere's employees: hats, clothing, awards, plant badges, watches, and many other things. Amazingly, relatively few of these survive to this day.

A large company like Deere employed many employees, and an easy means of identification was necessary at the many factories of Deere. This problem was solved by the issuance of Deere employee badges, of which there were quite a few different ones made, as each factory required its own. Security employees also merited an identification badge, and other specialty badges were issued as needed. These badges were made of metal and usually bore the name of the area of Deere that had issued them. The Waterloo tractor works, Des Moines works, Plow works, and other sites all had their own badges. The employee was assigned a number, which appeared on the badge.

Most workers at the plants where Deere actually manufactured the equipment also wore a uniform of some kind. Period photographs of Deere personnel operating the equipment wore what almost appears to be a lab coat. These items are almost never seen today, as the areas they were worn in were not conducive to keeping clothing clean. Most clothing

Two employee badges and an employee service necklace are shown. Note the leaping deer imprints and the two small emeralds.

Many technicians wore overalls as their uniform and besides sporting a deer logo on the front, many times the dealership name was embroidered on the back.

like this was destroyed or disposed of long ago. The few that have been collected are notable more for their survival than their actual value.

No matter how dedicated an employee was to Deere, eventually the day would come when it was time for him to retire. Deere has for years, and continues to this day, presented its employees with a small gold pin that certifies their years of employment at Deere. Men traditionally received a lapel pin or tie tack. Women received a necklace. The actual pin portion was the same on all of them. It bears the likeness of John Deere, and in many cases a small stone is set into it. An emerald signifies five years of service, a diamond 10 years. The

Two different employee badges have different employee numbers than the two in the first photograph. Additionally, the Deere & Mansur badge is identified as belonging to an office employee. *Melvin and Annette Warren*

A rare cast-iron deer bank like this one can be the centerpiece of a well-acquired John Deere collection. *Robert Duffel*

stone was added to the employee's pin as each milestone was achieved. This pin serves as a token of Deere's appreciation for the years served by an employee. Also, various sales, safety, and other awards have been presented over the years.

Prices

Item	Price
Badge, metal, "John Deere Security" wording, #8	$50.00
Badge, metal, four-legged deer logo w/ "John Deere Waterloo Works" wording/employee number, #8	75.00
Badge, metal, four-legged deer logo, w/"Van Brunt Mfg. Co" wording/ employee number, #8	85.00
Badge, metal, picture of John Deere w/ "John Deere Harvester Works" wording, #9	100.00
Badge, metal, picture of John Deere w/ "John Deere Ottumwa Works" wording/employee number, #3	35.00
Badge, metal, picture of John Deere w/ "John Deere Ottumwa Works" wording/employee number, #9	95.00
Bank, cast-iron deer, given as retirement gift, #9	600.00
Coat, lab style, serviceman's, white, four-legged deer logo on pocket, #3	35.00
Hat, cloth, serviceman's, dark green, four-legged logo w/ "John Deere Quality Farm Equipment" wording, #6	250.00
Hat, straw, child's, yellow w/green four-legged deer logo, #9	100.00
Hat, straw, Western, yellow w/green four-legged deer logo, #8	75.00
Jacket, serviceman's, dark green, four-legged deer logo on pocket, #6	50.00
Menu, retirement banquet, four-legged logo, 1956, #9	20.00
Necklace, service, gold w/picture of John Deere, two emeralds, #7	125.00
Overall, serviceman's, dark green, four-legged deer logo on breast, dealer's name embroidered on back, #5	50.00
Overall, serviceman's, dark green, four-legged deer logo on pocket, #8	150.00
Pin, lapel, service, gold w/ picture of John Deere, two emeralds, #8	100.00
Pin, lapel, service, gold w/picture of John Deere, no stones, #9	45.00
Pin, lapel, service, gold w/picture of John Deere, two rubies, #7	150.00
Shirt, bowling, white w/4-legged deer logo and dealer's name on back, #8	50.00

CHAPTER 23

SIGNS, FLAGS, AND PENNANTS

John Deere signs have been around as long as the company itself has been. Earliest signs were wooden and painted and have not survived the years very well. A few were even made from canvas on a wooden frame. Later signs were either tin or a heavy-gauge metal with enamel or porcelain on them. Other

Most early John Deere signs were similar to this sign. Rectangular in shape, the black, red, and yellow colors are brilliant even today. This sign measures 72x24 inches and features the four-legged deer logo. It was made by the Veribrite Sign Co. and has had a severe bend in the middle with amateur attempts at repair. Variations on this sign include three-legged deer logos, black deer logos, variations in wording, and even a 9-foot sign!

This sign's excellent condition causes it to reflect light far too easily. Once given to customers to mount on their buildings or fences, these tin signs were subject to the weather and buckshot. Most are either rusted away or damaged beyond repair.

This yellow-and-green oval shield is an NOS sign, but time has taken its toll, with the beginnings of rust becoming apparent. It has a wood frame, measures 58x42 inches, and was made by the Grace Sign Company.

This rectangular sign also shares the oval shield design and measures 58x42 inches. New also, it has experienced some shelf wear. Interestingly, it is made with reflective paint. It was also made by the Grace Sign Company.

popular materials that are commonly found today are cardboard, pressboard, and even plastic. The heavy metal signs have usually lasted quite nicely and remain bright and colorful to this day. A porcelain sign is easily chipped, though, and most have suffered at least a modicum of damage and many have a major bend in them.

The tin signs usually did not fare the passage of time as well. Often they are at least slightly rusty and perhaps even bent.

Traditionally, metal signs have captured the lion's share of collectors' interest but an increasing emphasis is developing on vintage neon signs. As with the others, neon signs can be somewhat the worse for wear as the elements were at times harsh on a neon's glass tubes and electrical components. The enameled surfaces have usually survived reasonably intact, but most surviving neon signs require at the bare minimum new neon tubes and repair to the electrics.

A great find, this large neon John Deere sign still resides in its original shipping crate. The attaching hardware is fastened inside the crate in a small canvas bag. Unbeatable!

Nice, painted fiberboard hardware sign. Correct era? Possibly not. Four-legged deer? You bet!

A rectangular dealer's sign, this was designed to be mounted in front of the dealership and lit up. The long-vanished dealer's name is still crisp and colorful. *Robert Duffel*

This 1950's vintage John Deere New & Used sign is mounted over the watchful eyes of another kind of deer.
Robert Duffel

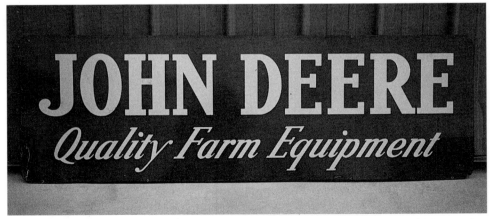

An unusual rectangular shape, this green with yellow lettering sign is a Canadian one. It measures 72x24 inches. A small stash of these was discovered by a Montana collector a few years ago.

Perhaps rarer than many signs, these paper pennants and flags were flown at fairs and on dealers' showroom floors. Touting the features and benefits of various pieces of John Deere equipment, they are very colorful and must have looked impressive when flown over a lineup of new two-cylinder tractors and machinery. Being paper, very, very few have survived.

Very similar in appearance to the sign on page 101, this sign is smaller and is a painted tin sign, not a porcelain steel sign. This is another interesting variation that makes this a desirable sign for collectors.

The cardboard and pressboard signs are easily damaged; water damage is perhaps the most difficult to deal with, as the material itself disintegrates. These signs also chip or bend and break easily. Plastic signs, although one of the newer materials to be used, are now reaching the age where the plastic itself can become discolored or brittle due to its age. Paint loss due to age is also commonly encountered on older plastic signs as the paint loses its adhesion. Of course, breakage and scratches are always a concern with a plastic sign too.

As with all items, condition is very important in determining current value. Truly uncommon signs, no matter their size, can command surprising amounts of money when sold. Most signs purchased by collectors are put on display where they can be enjoyed by their new owner and no doubt a few envious friends!

Prices

Item	Price
Pennants, cloth, green w/yellow 4-legged deer logo, 1950s, 34-foot string of pennants, NOS, very nice, #10	$150.00
Pennants, paper, green/yellow/red/white/orange, "John Deere" & multiple advertising slogan wording, 1930s, 14-foot string of pennants, NOS, rare, very nice, #10	500.00
Sign, canvas w/green wood frame, "The Light Running New John Deere" wording, 1910s–1920s, 15x60 inches, nice, #8	200.00
Sign, cardboard, yellow w/ "Buy Genuine John Deere Planter Runners Today" wording, pics of runner, 1950s, 17x17 inches, nice, #8	30.00
Sign, metal, black/white, "John Deere, Sacramento, Buggies, Implements" wording, 1900s, 10x20 inches, very nice, #9	350.00
Sign, metal, black w/red "Farm Implements" wording & black 4-legged deer logo, 1930s–1940s, 24x72 inches, rare, excellent, #9	2,000.00
Sign, metal, black w/yellow "Farm Equipment" wording, 4-legged deer logo, vertical double-sided sign, nice, #8	1,500.00
Sign, metal, black w/yellow/red "Farm Implements" wording, 3-legged deer logo, 1910s–1920s, 22x94 inches, nice, #8	600.00
Sign, metal, black w/yellow/red "Farm Implements" wording, 3-legged deer logo, 1920s, 24x84 inches, "VeriBrite" made, good, #7	600.00
Sign, metal, black w/yellow/red "Farm Implements" wording, 4-legged deer logo, 1930s, 24x72 inches, "VeriBrite" made, average, #5	250.00
Sign, metal, black w/yellow/red "Farm Implements" wording, 4-legged deer logo, 1930s, 24x72 inches, "Veribrite" made, very nice, #9	700.00
Sign, metal, green/yellow w/ "John Deere" wording in neon, double- sided, dealer name, 1930s–1940s, 40x72 inches, rough, #3	500.00
Sign, metal, green/yellow w/ "John Deere" wording in neon, double-sided, dealer name, 1930s–1940s, 40x72 inches, New In Crate, #10	5,000.00
Sign, metal, yellow w/black "Quality Farm Implements" wording, 3-legged deer logo, dealer name, 1930s, 12x23 inches, very nice, #9	400.00
Sign, metal, yellow/green "John Deere" wording, 4-legged deer logo, 1950s, good, #7	800.00
Sign, metal, yellow/green "New and Used" wording, 4-legged deer shield logo, 1950s, used equipment sign, vertical double-sided sign, nice, #8	500.00
Sign, metal, yellow/green w/ white "Buy Genuine John Deere Parts" wording, 4-legged deer shield logo, 1950s, 28x5 inches, #8	100.00
Sign, plastic, pole mount, lights, double-sided four-legged deer logo, 3x3 feet, dealer's sign, #7	2,500.00
Sign, plastic, pole mount, lights, double-sided four-legged deer logo, 6x6 feet, dealer's sign, #6	4,500.00
Sign, pressboard, JD Genuine Parts, black/yellow/white, nice, #8	85.00
Sign, pressboard, JD Hardware, 1950s, black/yellow/white, good, #7	35.00
Sign, wooden, silver w/ black "Fuel Dollar" wording, 1930s, 19 inches round x1 inch thick, edges notched to resemble coin, #8	600.00

CHAPTER 24
WATCHES, CLOCKS, AND FOBS

Watch fobs were made to fasten to pocket watches and usually consisted of a leather or cloth strap and a fob with some design or logo imprinted in it. John Deere soon began offering watch fobs with various Deere logos. The earliest fobs were not produced in the numbers that later fobs were, and the passing years have also taken their toll.

The pocket watch eventually gave way to the wristwatch as the timepiece of choice, and the production of fobs also slowed to a trickle of its former levels. The pocket watches themselves were often used by Deere as a token of extraordinary or faithful service. These watches were essentially presentation watches and were inscribed with the recipient's name and mention of why the watch was presented. They were usually presented upon occasion of an employee's retirement, noteworthy job performance, birthday, or other similar event.

One of the most sought-after clocks is the round clock known as the "Quality Farm Equipment" clock. This clock is

The "blue" or "cobalt blue" watch fob. This same design was also available in a turquoise, red/white/ blue, and black. *Melvin and Annette Warren*

15 inches in diameter and the clock face is a milk-white glass. The face features the four-legged leaping deer logo on a shield with the "Quality Farm Equipment" words in the bottom of the shield. The face is covered by a bubble glass that is fastened to the back by a metal retaining ring on the edge of the clock. The actual clock body is made of a synthetic material, perhaps bakelite or pressboard.

Recently, a very few vintage alarm clocks have surfaced with John Deere graphics on their face. There are also several different pocket watches with John Deere tractors for backgrounds that are questionable as to their authenticity as vintage pieces. These were likely either approved of or tolerated by Deere. Several of the tractor pocket watches are included in the pricing guide for informational purposes. The alarm clocks and pocket watches are both uncommon today.

This neat green-and-yellow four-legged deer clock is original to the author's dealership. It ran up until two years ago when it finally quit and was replaced by a vintage Farmhand brand clock. Future plans include repair and restoration.

Prices

Item	Price
Clock, alarm, metal, pics of Waterloo Boy tractor/Deere plow on face, made by Western, dated 1921, #7	$2,000.00
Clock, wall, rectangular electric, lights, green/yellow four-legged deer logo w/ "John Deere" wording on face of clock, clock to one side, "Parts" wording to other side of clock, composite body, 1950s, #8	800.00
Clock, wall, round electric, lights, green/yellow four-legged deer logo w/ "John Deere Quality Farm Equipment" wording on milk-glass face, composite body, 1950s, #8	800.00
Clock, wall, square electric, green/yellow four-legged deer logo w/ "John Deere" wording, 1950s, #8	600.00
Fob, watch, "Mother of Pearl" shield, leaping deer over plow, "antlers forward," w/leather strap/pearl buckle, chipped, #6	150.00
Fob, watch, "Mother of Pearl" shield, leaping deer over plow, "antlers forward," w/leather strap/metal buckle, #9	300.00
Fob, watch, "Mother of Pearl" shield, leaping deer over plow, "antlers backward," w/leather strap/pearl buckle, NOS on card, #10	300.00
Fob, watch, "Mother of Pearl" shield, leaping deer over plow, "antlers backward," w/leather strap/pearl buckle, NOS, no card, #10	230.00
Fob, watch, "Mother of Pearl" shield, leaping deer over plow, "antlers backward," w/leather/metal buckle, chipped, #7	175.00
Fob, watch, black shield, leaping deer over log, "John Deere" "Trademark" wording, w/leather strap/metal buckle, 1930s, #8	200.00
Fob, watch, bronze shield, leaping deer over plow, w/leather strap/metal buckle, #6	300.00
Fob, watch, bronze sunburst shield, leaping deer over log, "John Deere" "Trademark" wording, w/leather strap/metal buckle, 1930s, #8	200.00
Fob, watch, bronze, Waterloo Boy, w/leather strap/buckle, 1920s, #8	300.00
Fob, watch, celluloid Model D tractor, no strap or buckle, 1920s, #6	600.00
Fob, watch, celluloid Model D tractor, w/leather strap/buckle, 1920s, #8	1,000.00
Fob, watch, celluloid Waterloo Boy, picture of gas engine on one side, tractor on other, w/leather strap/metal buckle, 1910s, #8	1,800.00
Fob, watch, Centennial round bronze, picture of John Deere on one side, picture of plow and "John Deere Centennial" wording on other, no strap or buckle, 1937, #6	35.00
Fob, watch, Centennial round bronze, picture of John Deere on one side, picture of plow and "John Deere Centennial" wording on other, w/leather strap/pearl buckle, 1937, #8	200.00
Fob, watch, oval black, leaping deer over plow, w/leather strap/metal buckle, 1920s–1930s, #8	600.00
Fob, watch, oval dark blue, leaping deer over plow, w/leather strap/metal buckle, 1920s–1930s, #8	400.00
Fob, watch, oval red/white/blue, leaping deer over plow, w/leather strap/metal buckle, 1920s–1930s, #8	500.00
Fob, watch, oval turquoise blue, leaping deer over plow, w/leather strap/metal buckle, 1920s–1930s, #7	400.00
Fob, watch, Prairie Schooner, picture of John Deere on one side, picture of plow and prairie schooner on other, w/leather strap/metal buckle, 1930s–1940s, #7	150.00
Fob, watch, round silver, "D" logo w/deer head, "John Deere" wording, round, w/leather strap/metal buckle, #9	400.00
Fob, watch, round silver, "Moline Wagon" picture of running dog, w/leather strap and metal buckle, 1910s, #9	200.00
Watch, pocket, Model MT tractor, #8	60.00
Watch, pocket, Model R tractor, #7	50.00

CHAPTER 25

TOYS

John Deere actually made quite a few toys during the two-cylinder era. Around the early 1930s, the Vindex company was awarded the right to make Deere's first toys. The model D tractor, the first true all-Deere tractor, was also the first toy. Other toys made by Vindex included the spreader, thresher, wagons, combine, and plow. Vindex made these toys from cast iron, so while they lack the detail that we take for granted today, they were fairly durable, which accounts for the number that survive. Deere then appointed The Arcade Company to manufacture its toys. The model A tractor was its first offering and a wagon was next. World War II and a disastrous fire intervened in Arcade's toy ventures, and the company decided not to continue toy production after the war. Enter the Ertl company. Ertl began to produce Deere's toys and continues right up to this day. Ertl first made its own version of the model A tractor, changing it as time passed. The model B tractor was next, and then the model 60 tractor was released when Deere introduced the real tractor. A model 40 crawler was made at the same time. The models 620, 420 crawler, 630, 430, 430 crawler, and 440 crawler all followed. Two-cylinder toys ceased when the real tractors gave way to the New Generation series in 1960.

This toy ad from 1960 already featured the New Generation toy tractor, although some of the implements were the same ones available before the New Generation.

An original John Deere model A pedal tractor like this is impossible to find and priced like it! Dave Morrison

Imagine having this view in *your* basement! A vintage model A pedal tractor coming straight at you! Talk about lucky!
Dave Morrison

Toy tractors sold like wildfire, but a young farmer needed equipment to pull behind that toy. This spreader satisfied that need.

A model 60 pedal tractor with the black-knobbed noisemaker shifter. For some unknown reason, this noisemaker usually quit functioning very soon after the pedal tractor arrived! Too bad Dad could never quite get it fixed. *Dave Morrison*

The accepted beginning date for pedal tractors, although not sanctioned by Deere, was in 1948 when the Eska company produced what is today the rarest of all Deere pedal tractors. Although Deere never approved it, it was never painted green, and it never bore a John Deere decal, this pedal was obviously designed after the model A tractor and is commonly known as the "coffinblock" A. Deere finally approved the true model A pedal tractor in 1950. The "small" model 60 was next in 1952 and then the "large" model 60 in 1955. (The terminology refers to the differing size of the pedal tractors.) The model 620 sported the trademark yellow hood stripe and arrived in 1956. What is commonly referred to as the model 630 or 730, introduced in 1958, was actually the model 130 pedal tractor, but its design left no mistake as to what tractor it was styled after. The next pedal tractor would follow the shift away from two-cylinder tractors and was patterned on a New Generation tractor.

Prices

Item	Price
Ad, pedal tractor, model 50, 1950s, #8	$8.00
Ad, toys, later 1950s, #8	6.00
Toy, baler, model 14T, original/missing spring, 1950s, #8	85.00
Toy, baler, model 14T, restored, 1950s, #9	125.00
Toy, combine, model 12A, chipped, 1950s, #6	145.00
Toy, combine, model 12A, missing chain, 1950s, #8	100.00
Toy, combine, model 12A, restored, 1950s, #9	165.00
Toy, combine, model 30, chipped/missing chains/linkage, 1950s, #5	250.00
Toy, combine, model 30, restored, 1950s, #9	250.00

A staggering lineup of John Deere pedal tractors. Talk about eye candy! *Dave Morrison*

A toy tractor was also able to propel a pull-type combine. Note the canvas belt pickup and miniature chains.

Item	Price
Toy, disc, original w/ average box, 1950s, #7	225.00
Toy, dozer blade, worn, 1950s, #7	110.00
Toy, elevator, worn/broken conveyor, 1950s, #6	70.00
Toy, grain drill, restored, 1950s, #9	100.00
Toy, pedal tractor, "coffin block" model A, restored, 1940s, #10	20,000.00
Toy, pedal tractor, "large" model 60, 1950s, restored, #10	1,200.00
Toy, pedal tractor, "small" model 60, 1950s, restored, #10	1,100.00
Toy, pedal tractor, "small" model 60, broken body/missing wheels/steering/seat, 1950s, #3	300.00
Toy, pedal tractor, model 620, 1950s, restored, #10	1,400.00
Toy, pedal tractor, model 730 (130), 1950s, restored, #10	1,400.00
Toy, pedal tractor, model 730 (130), missing wheels/steering, #5	600.00
Toy, pedal tractor, model A, restored, 1950, #10	9,000.00
Toy, plow, 2-bottom, original, 1950s, #9	185.00
Toy, plow, 4-bottom, worn/bent, 1950s, #6	110.00
Toy, running gear, worn, 1950s, #6	25.00
Toy, spreader, original, 1950s, #8	75.00
Toy, tractor, model 40 crawler, green/yellow, chipped/missing tracks/broken levers, 1950s, #3	175.00
Toy, tractor, model 430 w/ 3 pt, green/yellow, 95% w/ good box, 1950s, #9	1,200.00
Toy, tractor, model 430 w/ 3 pt, green/yellow, chipped, 1950s, #7	450.00
Toy, tractor, model 430 w/ 3 pt, green/yellow, chipped/worn, 1950s, #5	500.00
Toy, tractor, model 430 w/ 3 pt, no paint/bent steering wheel/missing front wheel/bent hitch, #2	370.00
Toy, tractor, model 440 crawler, yellow, chipped/missing tracks, 1950s, #3	210.00
Toy, tractor, model 60 w/ loader, original, #8	500.00
Toy, tractor, model 60, green/yellow, 1950s, #8	165.00
Toy, tractor, model 60, green/yellow, chipped/broken muffler, 1950s, #6	75.00
Toy, tractor, model 60, green/yellow, chipped/missing steering wheel/bolts, 1950s, #6	65.00
Toy, tractor, model 60, green/yellow, restored, 1950s, #9	175.00
Toy, tractor, model 620 w/ 3 pt, chipped, 1950s, #7	130.00
Toy, tractor, model 620 w/ 3 pt, chipped/broken steering wheel/air stack, 1950s, #5	125.00
Toy, tractor, model 620 w/ 3 pt, chipped/missing steering wheel/broken lever/bent rear wheel, 1950s, #4	130.00
Toy, tractor, model 620 w/ 3 pt, original, 1950s, #8	190.00
Toy, tractor, model 620 w/ 3 pt, restored, 1950s, #9	245.00
Toy, tractor, model 620 w/ model 237 cornpicker, restored, 1950s, #9	500.00
Toy, tractor, model 630 w/ 3 pt, chipped/missing steering wheel/fenders, 1950s, #4	140.00
Toy, tractor, model 630 w/ 3 pt, original, 1950s, #8	200.00
Toy, tractor, model 630 w/ 3 pt, original, 1950s, #9	265.00
Toy, tractor, model 630 w/ 3 pt, restored, 1950s, #9	165.00
Toy, tractor, model A, Arcade tires/bent air stack, 1940s, #6	105.00
Toy, tractor, model A, chipped/missing front wheel, 1950s, #5	90.00
Toy, tractor, model A, chipped/missing front wheel/steering wheel/bent air stack, 1950s, #5	80.00
Toy, tractor, model hi-post A, bent air stack, 1950s, #7	125.00
Toy, tractor, model hi-post A, chipped, 1950s, #8	150.00
Toy, tractor, model hi-post A, restored, 1950s, #9	150.00
Toy, tractor, model hi-post A, w/ good box, 1950s, #9	500.00
Toy, tractor, Vindex model D, 1930s, #7	1,200.00
Toy, wagon, Arcade, original, 1930s, #8	500.00

CHAPTER 26
MATCHBOOKS, ASHTRAYS, AND LIGHTERS

John Deere dealers were only too happy to keep a supply of free matchbooks on hand to pass out to area farmers, imprinted with the dealer's name, of course! That way, each time Mr. Farmer paused during his day to light one up, a subtle message regarding John Deere tractors and the local dealer was passed on as the cigarette was coaxed to life.

Many different styles and types of matchbooks, ashtrays, and lighters were produced. Some were fairly plain and utilitarian while others were quite ornate. As matches were made to be used up and were also made of paper, most have disappeared long ago, making remaining examples quite sought after. Ashtrays were usually used heavily and most had at least minor damage to the imprint from the heat of the cigarettes and matches. Lighters suffered from the effects of hard use and were usually used until they wore out. This makes these difficult to find today in presentable condition. Factor in the variety of styles and imprints and these are all fun items to add to one's collection.

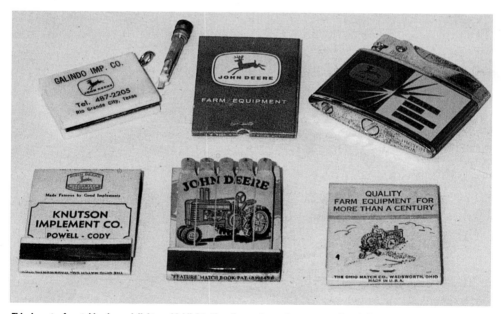

This layout of matchbooks and lighters highlights the diverse types that were produced. The upper left-hand corner features a mechanical match, while the matches in the lower center actually have a two-cylinder tractor picture printed on their covers. Colorful and collectible. *Melvin and Annette Warren*

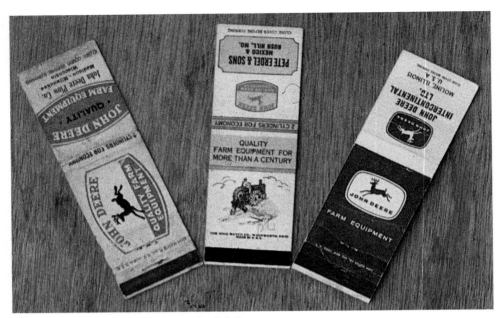

Another view of some matchbooks. *Greg Stephen/Bob Key*

Prices

Item	Price
Ashtray, ceramic, black, square, dealer name, 1940s, #8	$30.00
Ashtray, copper, raised leaping deer/John Deere/plow, large, #6	250.00
Ashtray, glass, green/yellow dealer name, logo, #9	28.00
Ashtray, metal, black, dealer name, shaped like coal bucket, #7	15.00
Ashtray, metal, galvanized, round, logo imprint, Van Brunt grain drill material sample ashtray, #8	35.00
Ashtray, metal, red, combo John Deere/Dodge/Plymouth wording, #4	20.00
Lighter, green, clear plastic, tractor picture, "JD Dubuque Tractor Works, Dubuque, IA" wording, 1950s, #10, rare	100.00
Lighter, metal, Bleb, green/yellow sunburst enamel design, 4-legged logo in gold, "Sparks New Farming Power" wording, 1950s, #7	45.00
Lighter, metal, red wrinkle finish, raised 1930s logo, #8, rare	50.00
Lighter, metal, Zip, raised logo, engraved name, 1950s, #10	40.00
Lighter, metal, Zip, raised tractor picture, raised logo, 1950s, #5	18.00
Matchbook, green/yellow, dealer name, 4-legged deer logo, 1950s, #8	8.00
Matchbook, green/yellow, large 4-legged deer logo, "Virtue Fertilizer," #5	28.00
Matchbook, large logo, "Iowa State Fair 1939" wording, #8	15.00
Matchbook, red, JD Company Centennial logo-1937, #8	20.00
Matchbook, white/green/yellow, dealer name, 2 tractor picture, 1940s, #9	12.00
Matchbook, white/green/yellow, large matchbook, dealer name, logo, 1950s, #8	10.00
Matchbook, white/yellow/green, dealer name, tractor picture, 1940s, #5	8.00
Matchbook, yellow, reusable mechanical match, dealer name, 1950s, #10	25.00
Matchbook, yellow/green, 2 logos, tractor picture on matches, 1940s, #10	22.00
Matchbook, yellow/green, dealer name, 4-legged deer logo, 1940s, #5	8.00
Matchbook, yellow/green, dealer name, 4-legged deer logo, 1940s, #8	12.00
Matchbook, yellow/green, dealer name, tractor picture, 1950s, no matches, #3	6.00
Matchbook, yellow/green, tractor picture, no name, 1940s, #7	10.00

CHAPTER 27

JEWELRY, PINS, AND KNIVES

Hats, shirts, jackets, coffee cups, and many more items all carry the Deere brand. The general theory is that if the Deere logo is everywhere, in everyday use, then overall Deere awareness is increased or enhanced. Deere produced many items of a personal nature, such as jewelry, meant to be used by farmers and their families who wanted to fashionably display their brand preference.

For the two-cylinder period we are discussing, the examples that follow show that the company offered a significant amount of jewelry. Of course, it pales in comparison to what has been offered the last 30 years or so. Pity the future collector who decides to collect even just belt buckles!

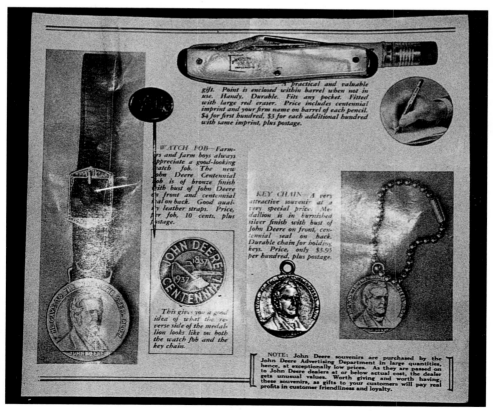

This original memento order form is in remarkable condition. Displayed against it are a well-worn pocketknife, a key chain medallion, and a Velie brand stickpin.

A great collection of four-legged deer key chains. *Robert Duffel*

Prices

Item	Price
Button, celluloid, four-legged deer logo, #6	$45.00
Button, celluloid, John Deere Plow Co., deer head logo, #8	225.00
Button, celluloid, Waterloo Boy, picture of boy and tractor, #8	200.00
Coin purse, gold sparkle plastic, dealer name/four-legged logo in black, #8	20.00
Key chain, centennial medallion, complete w/chain, #8	35.00
Key chain, centennial medallion, worn, no attaching ring or chain, #3	10.00
Key chain, prairie schooner, complete w/chain, #8	35.00
Key chain, rectangular yellow four-legged deer logo, #9	35.00
Key chain, round clear w/ green/yellow four-legged deer logo, #9	35.00
Key chain, round w/ yellow four-legged deer, #8	25.00
Key chain, silver, four-legged deer logo, #7	18.00
Key chain, yellow rectangular plastic w/green red legged deer logo, #9	30.00
Knife, brass handle, 2 blades, four-legged deer logo/LANZ name, #7	200.00
Knife, pearl handle, unusual round, four-legged deer logo, dealer name, #6	35.00
Knife, pearl handle, white/green, four-legged deer logo, dealer name, #6	20.00
Knife, white handle, green wording "John Deere Plow Co.," #8	95.00
Money clip, green four-legged deer on gold background, #9	50.00
Money clip, silver four-legged deer on black background, #8	45.00
Pin, "D," blue border, deer over log logo, gold plated, #8	125.00
Pin, bronze shield, deer over log logo, "John Deere Plow Co." wording, #8	150.00
Pin, green four-legged deer logo on gold background, #8	35.00
Pin, gold four-legged deer logo on green background, #8	35.00
Pin, likeness of John Deere, bronze color, #7	65.00
Pin, stick, leaping deer over a log, gold plated, no pin, #3	8.00
Pin, stick, leaping deer over a log, gold plated, #7	35.00
Pin, stick, leaping deer over a log, gold plated, excellent, #10	45.00
Pin, stick, leaping deer over a log, gold plated, pin bent, worn, #5	12.00
Pin, stick, Moline Plow, #7	100.00
Pin, stick, Velie, bronze color, #7	65.00
Pin, walking plow, gold plated, #6	25.00
Pin, walking plow, gold plated, excellent, #10	45.00
Pin, Waterloo Boy, bronze color, #8	100.00
Tie, bolo, brass four-legged deer logo clasp, #8	75.00
Tie, bolo, rectangular brass w/green four-legged logo, #8	75.00

CHAPTER 28
CUPS, NAPKINS, SALT & PEPPER SHAKERS, AND JOHN DEERE DAY ITEMS

John Deere dealers have traditionally thrown at least one special event or open house once a year. Different items, ranging from advertisements to invitations to incentives, were made to promote and facilitate a John Deere Day through the years. Also, dealers from time to time would sponsor sales meetings to launch a new model of equipment, and usually some form of refreshment was available. John Deere wasted no time in providing the dealers, for a nominal charge, Deere imprinted disposable dinnerware for their use whenever providing a meal to customers. Dealers have, over the years, had their names printed on virtually any item that was available. Salt and pepper shakers, pitchers, tablecloths, centerpieces, anything that might further circulate the dealership's name. This variety, and the variations in artwork as the years passed, is what makes these another fun item to collect.

Similar and yet different, each of these two cups has a unique slogan.

A close-up of the napkin. There were various designs over the years, and John Deere continues supplying paper cups and napkins to this day.

These four cups are all different, yet share the four-legged logo, as does the napkin.

Prices

Item	Price
Cup, 4-legged logo, white w/green wording and stripes, #8	$7.00
Cup, coffee, 4-legged logo, white w/ dealer name, #6	6.00
Cup, white/green JD wording, paper, fold-out handles, #9	8.00
Glass, clear w/ black pattern/4-legged logo/tractor pics, #8	35.00
JD Day advertisement, 4-legged logo, no imprint, #8	15.00
JD Day invitation w/ticket, 4-legged logo, dealer name, #7	22.00
JD Day sign, small, 4-legged logo, dealer name, #8	20.00
JD Day ticket, blue, 4-legged logo, dealer name, #9	25.00
JD Day ticket, yellow, 4-legged logo, dealer name, #8	25.00
Napkin, 4-legged logo, white/green wording, picture of thirty series tractor, #9	8.00
Napkin, 4-legged logo, white/green, #8	7.00
Napkin, 4-legged shield logo, white/green/yellow w/green stripes, #9	8.00
Shaker, Salt & Pepper, combo, orange w/black John Deere/dealer name, #10	20.00
Shaker, Salt & Pepper, combo, yellow w/4-legged logo, #8	15.00
Shaker, Salt & Pepper, glass, 4-legged logo, #7	15.00
Shaker, Salt & Pepper, white ceramic, 4-legged logo/dealer name, #8	15.00

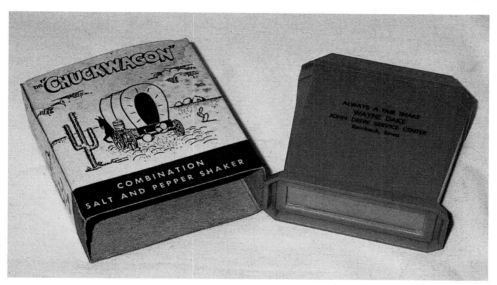

Orange seems out of place on John Deere salt and pepper shakers! *Melvin and Annette Warren*

CHAPTER 29

PENS AND PENCILS

John Deere dealers were supplying free pens or pencils as giveaways many, many years ago. Every time the farmer would jot a note in his notebook, the dealer felt it was best done with a John Deere green and yellow writing instrument! There have been literally hundreds and hundreds of variations on pens and pencils over the years. Many featured current slogans or even pictures of current tractors or machinery, but the two things that every one of them had was the John Deere leaping deer logo and the dealer's name. These are some of the items that have been collected the longest, as every dealer had a different one to offer. Most changed designs at least every

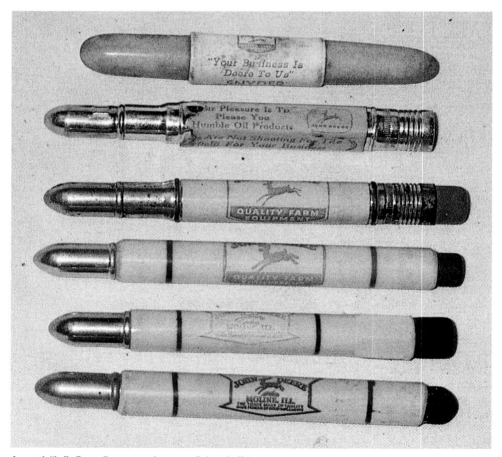

Assorted "bullet" pencils, no two the same. *Robert Duffel*

Deere has created endless variations of the pen and pencil set over the years. This particular set is a John Deere Ottumwa Works set and is branded with the four-legged deer logo. *Dave Morrison*

other year, so there was quite a diversity to choose from. They have been made of many materials and finishes over the years. Wood, plastic, metal, painted, etched, engraved, pearlized, chromed, brass plated, clear plastic, rubberized, and on and on. It is sometimes difficult to find two examples of a certain desirable pen or pencil, as the attrition rate was so high. Although you might think that the most desirable imprints would be of dealers long gone, it seems as if a pen or pencil is especially prized if it carries the name of a dealer still in business these many years later.

Prices

Item	Price
Pen, black plastic bottom, silver metal upper, silver 4-legged logo, #9	$18.00
Pen, green bottom, gold metal upper, w/dealer name/tractor picture, #8	8.00
Pen, green plastic bottom, pearlized upper, w/dealer name, #7	4.00
Pen, green plastic bottom, yellow plastic upper, yellow 4-legged logo, #9	12.00
Pen, silver metal, green 4-legged logo on pocket clip, #10	25.00
Pen, white bottom, gold metal upper, w/dealer name/tractor picture, #6	4.00
Pen, white plastic bottom, silver metal upper, green 4-legged logo, #10	15.00
Pen, yellow plastic bottom, gold metal upper w/green stripes/logo/dealer name, #8	8.00
Pen, yellow plastic bottom, green upper, yellow clicker, yellow 4-legged log, #7	5.00
Pencil, "Bullet," green 4-legged logo/dealer name, #7	19.00
Pencil, "Bullet," white body w/red stripes, green 4-legged logo, dealer name, #6	18.00
Pencil, "Bullet," white body w/red stripes, green deer over log shield logo, dealer name, hexagonal body end by eraser, #8	25.00
Pencil, "Bullet," yellow body w/red stripes, green deer over log shield logo, dealer name, #7	16.00
Pencil, black plastic body, yellow can top w/green 4-legged logo, dealer name, #6	8.00
Pencil, black plastic bottom, silver metal upper, silver 4-legged logo, #9	18.00
Pencil, green plastic bottom, pearlized upper w/ 4-legged logo/dealer name, #8	20.00
Pencil, later "Bullet," yellow body, green 4-legged logo, dealer name, #9	28.00
Pencil, later square-body "Bullet," yellow body, green 4-legged logo, dealer name, Humble Oil logo, green wording, #6	16.00
Pencil, pearlized body, w/green 4-legged logo/dealer name, #7	18.00
Pencil, red bottom, gold metal upper, black 3-legged logo, dealer name, #6	12.00
Pencil, silver metal, green 4-legged logo on pocket clip, #10	25.00
Pencil, white plastic body, green caps, green 4-legged logo/dealer name, wording, #7	20.00
Pencil, yellow body, green 4-legged logo/tractor picture/dealer name, #9	25.00

This last chapter is for items different from the other categories. As mentioned throughout this book, Deere has
made items nearly too numerous to count. The following items
vary from others listed elsewhere in this book but were judged
interesting enough to merit inclusion in this final chapter. They
range from very old and very valuable items to items of little or
no importance save for bearing the John Deere name. They are
intriguing due to the very fact that this chapter, more than any

This glass paperweight
is far older than it
looks. The item
underneath it is an
honest-to-goodness *new*
model H tractor serial
number plate! It has
never been marked!
Wonderful additions to
any collection.

other, illustrates the wide variety of items that have borne the John Deere logo. This variety is the strength of this hobby.

Prices

Item	Price
Bag, fertilizer 45-0-0, 50 lb., empty, four-legged logo, 1950s, #7	$50.00
Spoons, measuring w/rack, four-legged logo w/dealer name, 1950s, #8	25.00
Umbrella, yellow w/green four-legged logo/ "John Deere" wording, worn, #5	35.00
Umbrella, yellow w/green four-legged logo/ "John Deere" wording, #8	100.00
Umbrella, six point, yellow w/black "John Deere" wording, metal pole, #8	200.00
Broom, whisk, "John Deere-Delaval-Maytag" wording, #8	50.00
Paperweight, cast-iron deer, "John Deere" wording, 1920s, #7	400.00
Paperweight, glass, "John Deere Plow Company-Kansas City, MO" wording, "D" w/ deer head logo, #8	500.00
Paperweight, Centennial, metal, picture of John Deere, #8	125.00

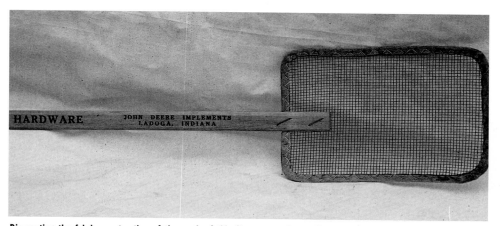

Discounting the fabric construction of the mesh of this fly swatter, the wording "John Deere Implements" alone identifies it as dating from the 1910s to the 1920s.

The John Deere "Double Copper Penny" dealer's medallion, given only to dealers in 1937 to commemorate Deere's 100th anniversary. Deere waited until 1987 to do something similar when it gave dealers a 150th anniversary medallion plaque.

The golden yellow and black color scheme identifies this tractor medallion's origin as an industrial piece of equipment. Still a four-legged deer, though!

Item	Price
Hanging, wall, double round, Centennial, copper-colored "Double Penny," given to dealers in 1937, picture of John Deere on one, picture of plow on other, rare, #10	1,000.00
Game, ball in hole, picture of Model A tractor on face, "John Deere Quality Farm Equipment" wording w/dealer name, 1950s, #8	125.00
Record, 45 rpm, "John Deere ballad," four-legged logo, 1950s, #8	25.00
Balloon, yellow w/green four-legged logo/ "John Deere" wording, dealer name, has two holes for attaching, #8	15.00
Opener, letter, brass, "Velie" on one side, "Deere" on other, #8	50.00
Measure, tape, celluloid, green w/yellow, bust of John Deere, #8	125.00
Measure, tape, celluloid, green w/yellow, four-legged deer logo, #8	125.00
Measure, tape, metal, four-legged deer logo, #8	150.00
Brush, celluloid, round, green w/yellow, bust of John Deere, dated 1924, #9	450.00
Brush, celluloid, oval, green w/yellow, bust of John Deere, 1920s, #7	300.00
Gauge, hardware, metal, four-legged deer logo, 1950s, #8	15.00
Bank, Centennial, green w/yellow, coffee-can shaped, 1937, #9	200.00
Fan, fold-open, four-legged deer logo, dealer name, #7	35.00
Plate, license plate, yellow w/ "John Deere-Chevrolet" wording, #9	100.00
Bag, fertilizer, 24-12-12, 50 lb., empty, four-legged logo, 1950s, #7	35.00

APPENDIX

Resources

Following are various resources that collectors may want to avail themselves of if they desire further information.

John Deere Related–Magazines

The Green Magazine, RR1, Bee, NE 68314

Two Cylinder, Box 219, Grundy Center, IA 50638

Antique Power, Box 562, Yellow Springs, OH 45387

The Belt Pulley, 20114 Illinois Rt 16, Nokomis, IL 62075

Polk's Antique Tractor Magazine, 72435 SR 15, New Paris, IN 46553

Gas Engine Magazine, Box 328, Lancaster, PA 17608

Engineers & Engines, 2240 Oak Leaf St., Box 2757, Joliet, IL 60434

Toy Farmer, 7496 106th Ave SE, LaMoure, ND 58458

Online Auctions

www.ebay.com

www.yahoo.com

www.amazon.com

Websites

www.atis.net

www.ytmag.com

www.theoldtractorcompany.com